Major Studies of Minority Business

MAJOR STUDIES OF MINORITY BUSINESS

A Bibliographic Review

Timothy Bates

Joint Center for Political and Economic Studies Press
Washington, D.C.

Joint Center for Political and Economic Studies, Inc.

The Joint Center for Political and Economic Studies contributes to the national interest by helping black Americans participate fully and effectively in the political and economic life of our society.

A nonpartisan, nonprofit institution founded in 1970, the Joint Center uses research and information dissemination to accomplish three objectives: to improve the socioeconomic status of black Americans; to increase their influence in the political and public policy arenas; and to facilitate the building of coalitions across racial lines.

Library of Congress Cataloging-in-Publication Data

Bates, Timothy Mason.
Major studies of minority business : a bibliographic review /
Timothy Bates.
p. cm.
Includes indexes.
1. Minority business enterprises—United States—Bibliography.
2. Small business—United States—Bibliography. I. Title.
Z7164.C81B33 1993
[HD2346.U5]
016.3386'422'0973—dc20 92–28391 CIP

ISBN 1–880285–03–7 (cloth : alk. paper)

© 1993, Joint Center for Political and Economic Studies, Inc.
1090 Vermont Avenue, N.W.
Suite 1100
Washington, D.C. 20005-4961

Distributed by arrangement with
University Press of America, Inc.
4720 Boston Way
Lanham, MD 20706

3 Henrietta Street
London WC2E 8LU England

Contents

Preface

In January 1989, the U.S. Supreme Court dealt a major blow to public officials striving to assure minority entrepreneurs a fair share of public contracts. The ruling in *Richmond* v. *Croson* struck down a minority set-aside program instituted by Richmond, Virginia, in 1983 to remedy discrimination. The ruling raised fears that governments would abandon set-asides and return to business as usual, a mode of operation that has historically short-changed minority companies.

In late 1989, the Joint Center for Political and Economic Studies, with support from the Ford Foundation, initiated a project to review policies designed to redress discrimination and unequal access to economic opportunity in American society and to provide information that would facilitate the development of new or revised policies in the area of group-sensitive remedies. This review is one of the products of that effort.

Jurisdictions that want to institute or redesign preferential programs for minority businesses have to produce evidence of discrimination against these firms. In addition, public support for the programs can be bolstered if there is evidence of communitywide benefits from the formation and expansion of minority businesses. One source for evidence of these communitywide benefits is the extensive literature on minority business development.

Over the past two decades, a small cadre of researchers and policy analysts have completed empirical studies of minority business development that have made significant contributions to our understanding of minority business formation and the obstacles to the growth of minority entrepreneurship. In early 1990, the Joint Center commissioned Timothy Bates, a noted scholar in the field, to prepare a bibliographic review that would make that knowledge accessible to the government officials, policy analysts, and consultants who are working on new policies for minority business development. The resulting publication is both comprehensive and timely. It makes a valuable contribution to the literature in this field.

For their editorial and design work on this volume we extend thanks to staff members Constance Toliver, Marc DeFrancis, Tyra Wright, and Allison King, who contributed under the able direction of communications director Nancy Stella.

Eddie N. Williams
President
Joint Center for Political
and Economic Studies

About the Author

An economist with a national reputation in the field of minority business development, Timothy Bates has written numerous articles in the leading economic and policy journals. He has written and coauthored several books, including *The Political Economy of the Urban Ghetto* (1984); *Financing Black Economic Development* (1979); and *Black Capitalism: A Quantitative Analysis* (1973).

For his expertise in minority entrepreneurship, Bates has been called to testify before federal agencies on several occasions. He was an American Statistical Association research fellow in 1988, and in 1989 was a visiting scholar at the Joint Center for Political and Economic Studies. He currently chairs the Urban Policy Analysis Graduate Program at the New School for Social Research in New York.

Introduction

Overview

Minority-owned businesses, traditionally concentrated in the small-scale retail and personal service sectors, were historically an obscure sector of the economy. Then, in the late 1960s, the federal government initiated programs to promote the expansion of black (and later, minority) businesses, and the programs proliferated well into the 1980s. Whereas most promotion efforts in the 1960s consisted of increasing the availability of loans, in the 1970s, efforts turned to targeting procurement dollars and "set-asides" toward minorities. Large corporations in the consumer products industries began to target procurement dollars toward minority firms, advertise in minority-owned publications, and deposit funds in minority-owned banks. In the 1980s, local governments began to use set-asides, and they continue to use them today. The latter reflects the growing political power of blacks (and Hispanics) in many central cities, who are now in positions to award contracts to minorities.

Whereas the traditional minority business community consisted predominantly of very small firms serving minority clienteles, in recent years, expanding market opportunities have induced minority entrepreneurs to create larger firms oriented toward corporate and government clienteles. Opportunities created by set-asides, preferential procurement policies, and the like have encouraged better educated, younger entrepreneurs to create and expand businesses in finance, insurance, real estate, contracting, wholesaling, manufacturing, and business services. Entrepreneurs in these emerging lines of business are not only younger and better educated, on average, than other self-employed minorities, but their earnings are higher. Although the traditional personal service and small-scale retail fields still account for a larger number of firms than the combined total of the above emerging lines of business, the owners in the traditional areas have, on average, lower education and earnings levels, and particularly in personal services, they are in a state of continuous decline.

Since the 1960s, the minority business community has started to diversify and expand in response to an influx of talent and capital. Nonetheless, it continues to lag behind the nonminority small business universe, because of several constraints placed on it. First of all, although access to financial capital has expanded since the 1960s, it is still severely constrained for minority entrepreneurs, particularly black ones. In addition, the constitutionality of minority business assistance programs is being challenged, and this threatens to reverse the process of expansion and diversification. Minority business set-asides at the state and local levels need to be reoriented in light of the judicial constraints imposed on set-aside programs by the Supreme Court's *Richmond* v. *Croson* ruling.

Another constraint is geographically related: inner-city black communities are increasingly being left out of the business development process.

Modern-day social scientists tend to overlook certain types of constraints on minority business activity. Quantitative studies, by their very nature, ignore problems that are not amenable to direct measurement. Most of the studies summarized in this bibliography relied on voluntary responses to questions posed by data collection agencies such as the U.S. Bureau of the Census. Individuals and institutions rarely respond that they discriminate against minorities; sometimes discriminatory patterns can be inferred from their responses and sometimes they cannot. The inability to measure discrimination in statistical terms does not necessarily mean that discriminatory behavior is absent.

The Nature of This Bibliography

Of the many hundreds of articles and books describing studies that analyzed minority self-employment, this bibliography reviews 99 works. Twelve of them are historic studies that examined minority business in the pre-World War II period; the remaining 87 focused on minority business problems and prospects in the post-World War II period.

Minority business studies can be sorted broadly into three fairly distinct types: (1) analyses of government programs that seek to assist and promote minority business, (2) analyses of minority business owners as individuals and the traits of the firms they operate, and (3) analyses of the impacts of minority businesses on others—clients, employees, and so forth. Although type number two dominates in the general literature, all three types are covered in this bibliography.

Several of the studies included apply to small businesses in general (see Part 2). They were chosen very selectively, and in every instance they apply greatly to minority business problems and prospects. In addition, several studies were selected because they describe factors that shaped the minority business milieu, such as educational trends, wealth holdings, commercial bank behavior, and traits of low-income ghetto communities. Thus, not every section of this bibliography directly discusses minority business, but every section contributes to understanding minority firms and the environment in which they operate.

The contents and conclusions of many studies of minority business are duplicative. In an effort to minimize duplication, I excluded from my review numerous studies. In choosing publications to review I was guided by three criteria. First, I gave studies published in easily accessible journals and books priority over studies presented in less accessible forms such as reports to government agencies and limited circulation discussion papers. Second, I gave studies that used statistical techniques to analyze large data bases priority over those that relied on anecdotal information, a few case studies, or secondhand information. Finally, I gave preference to more recent studies over older studies when topical coverage was similar; thus, selections have sometimes been made based on my evaluation of the relative merits of similar studies. Applying these three criteria led me to reject several hundred studies of minority business, including over 20 that I authored.

Some studies that are not easily accessible are nonetheless included in this bibliography because they contribute unique material that is not replicated in other more readily available articles and books. Studies that rely on secondhand information and anecdotal evidence were sometimes chosen for inclusion if they filled important gaps in our knowledge of minority enterprise.

Several resources that complement this bibliography are available to readers who wish to pursue minority business studies in greater depth. An overlapping bibliography is "Abstracts of the Sociological Literature on Minority Business Ownership," by Frank Fratoe (1984), a volume which does not discuss minority-owned financial institutions in depth. Good summary discussions of studies analyzing relevant financial institutions appear in "Black Banks: A Survey and Analysis of the Literature," by John Cole, Alfred Edwards, Earl Hamilton, and Lucy Reuben (1985), and in chapters 2 through 6 of *Financing Black Economic Development*, by Timothy Bates and William Bradford (1979), which is reviewed in this volume.

The reader may find it useful to refer to the three appendices that conclude this bibliography. Appendix A, "Historical Overview: The Black Business Community Before World War II," reviews the development of black business from prior to the Civil War to World War II. Appendix B, "Data Bases Used in the Studies," describes in detail the data bases that are mentioned briefly in the summaries of individual studies. Appendix C, "Glossary of Technical Terms," defines technical terms and statistical techniques that are referred to in this bibliography.

Early Studies

Minority-Owned Businesses

Widespread interest in minority business was clearly a product of the 1960s milieu and initially focused on black self-employment. Heightened awareness of the plight of blacks and their potential to disrupt urban areas led interest groups to endorse numerous black economic development programs. A large body of literature focusing on black business ownership emerged very quickly. This literature is discussed quite selectively in this section, since many of the studies were nonanalytical and repetitive. Authors often based their remarks on a small number of incidents or attempted to promote some policy to improve the environment for black business.

The early, comprehensive study of the black business community by Joseph Pierce (see entry no. 1, the first study reviewed in this volume) set the standard for several of the more informative analyses conducted in the 1960s. Pierce provided a descriptive analysis of the state of black business communities in 12 cities in 1944. According to Pierce, most black-owned firms were crowded into several small-scale personal service and retail lines of business. The self-employed blacks in these 12 cities said that the major barrier to black business was the limited access to financial capital. Later studies by Eugene Foley (no. 2) and by Richard Farmer (no. 3) were based on similar surveys of urban black-owned firms, and their findings suggested that the black business community of the mid-1960s had not progressed beyond the situation in the 1940s as described by Pierce.

A second type of study is also summarized in this section. David Caplovitz (no. 4) and Kent Gilbreath (no. 5) examined minority business from the sociologist's perspective. Caplovitz compared numerous personal traits of self-employed blacks and whites who were operating businesses in central Harlem. Gilbreath focused his analysis on native Americans, reflecting the broadening of interest in minority groups (other than blacks) in the early 1970s. Navajo culture, he argued, impedes the development of small business.

The third and final group of studies analyzed in this section put forth theories to explain past, present, and future behavior of black-owned businesses. In several studies, Andrew Brimmer (nos. 6a, 6b, 8a, and 8b) argued that discrimination and segregation benefit existing black-owned businesses by providing a protected market. According to his theory, the decline of segregation exposed black businesses to greater competition from nonminority businesses, and thus lessened their prospects for growth and profitable operation. In contrast, Bates (nos. 7, 9, and 10) argued that the decline of discrimination opened up opportunities for black businesses in areas where blacks had traditionally been restricted from competing on an equal basis. Small Business Administration loan programs greatly expanded the access of black firms to financial capital in the late 1960s. The Bates studies examined data from these programs, which showed that the increased access to financial capital enabled many black entrepreneurs to break away from the traditional lines of small, labor intensive, service oriented business enterprises. Finally, Robert Browne (no. 11) argued that black-owned neighborhood businesses strengthen the flow of income within the ghetto economy, creating local multiplier effects that generate jobs for area residents. Browne's ideas about the impact of minority-owned business development inspired studies that are reviewed in later sections of this bibliography.

1. Joseph Pierce.
Negro Business and Business Education.
New York: Harper and Brothers, 1947.

• This pioneering study is a comprehensive overview of the state of the urban black business community in 1944. In scope and substantive findings, the Pierce study stood as the definitive work in the field until the 1970s. Pierce described the black business universe of 1944 as one consisting largely of very small firms crowded into a few industry sectors.

His survey covered 12 cities across the country: eight in the South, two in the East, and two in the Midwest. He found 3,866 black-owned firms. Six types dominated, accounting for nearly 70 percent of the 3,866 firms:

Type of business	Number of firms
1. Beauty parlors and barber shops	1,004
2. Eating places	627
3. Groceries	491
4. Cleaning and pressing shops	288
5. Shoe shine and repair shops	130
6. Funeral parlors	126

The businesses in this list are strikingly similar to those that blacks operated in the antebellum South (see Appendix A). Among the retail establishments covered in Pierce's survey, 68.1 percent were either restaurants or grocery stores. The most common remaining lines of retailing were drug stores, gas stations, and taverns, which accounted for 5.3, 4.6, and 4.1 percent, respectively, of the black-owned retail establishments.

Pierce formed a subsample consisting of the firms in nine cities, for which he collected information on initial financial capitalization, age of the firm, and the problems identified by the owners as barriers to succeeding in business. The percentages of black-owned businesses initially capitalized at various amounts are reported below:

Initial capitalization amount	Percentage of firms capitalized at that amount
Less than $100	15.8
$100 - $400	25.2
$400 - $1000	23.4
$1000 - $5000	27.6
$5000 and up	8.0

The median value of initial capitalization was a low $549. The most frequent source of initial capitalization was personal savings, which was used by 86.3 percent of the owners; the second most frequent source of capital was family, used by 4.8 percent of the owners. Black-owned banks operated in five of the nine cities, but bank loans

7

was used by 8.6 percent of the owners; the second most frequent source of capital was family, used by 4.8 percent of the owners. Black-owned banks operated in five of the nine cities, but bank loans provided initial financial capital for only 3.3 percent of the firms, and the median bank loan amount was only $500. The median age of the firms was 5.3 years in retailing and 7.1 years in services. Of the six major lines of black business, funeral parlors had the highest median age (22.6 years), whereas shoe shine and repair shops had the lowest median age (3.2 years).

When asked to rank the most significant obstacles to progressive business operation among blacks, the entrepreneurs ranked the lack of financial capital as the greatest obstacle. Personnel problems ranked second and a lack of Negro patronage was third.

2. Eugene Foley. "The Negro Businessman: In Search of a Tradition." In *The Negro American*, edited by Talcott Parsons and Kenneth B. Clark. Boston: Houghton Mifflin, 1966.

• Foley described a comprehensive 1964 survey conducted by the Drexel Institute that encompassed virtually every black-owned firm in Philadelphia. The Drexel Institute located 4,242 black-owned firms, 9 percent of the city's total number of small businesses. The firms were typically very small and were concentrated in personal services and retailing, most commonly in beauty parlors and barbershops (35 percent) and restaurants (11 percent). Only 13 of the 4,242 firms were manufacturers and only 14 were wholesalers. The findings of the Drexel Institute survey were quite similar to those reported by Joseph Pierce in the 1940s: Black firms remained concentrated in the same lines of business as they were in during Pierce's study, and mean sales growth had barely outpaced inflation.

3. Richard T. Farmer. "Black Businessmen in Indiana." *Indiana Business Review* 43 (November 1968).

• Farmer gathered data on 130 of the estimated 200 black-owned businesses operating in Gary, Indiana, in 1968. Like the Drexel survey did in 1964, Farmer simply re-affirmed the black business pattern reported by Pierce in his 1944 survey. None of the businesses surveyed by Farmer were engaged in manufacturing; however, several wholesalers were operating. Most of the firms were tiny and provided services or sold goods. Owners complained most commonly about the inability to obtain credit.

4. David Caplovitz. *The Merchants of Harlem: A Study of Small Business in the Black Community.* **Beverly Hills, Calif.: Sage Publications, 1973.**

• Caplovitz interviewed 259 retail business owners in central Harlem in 1968 to compare the business experiences and social backgrounds of black and white businesspersons. He found that white owners, on average, had more experience in the business world. They tended to be older, had higher levels of education, were more likely to have owned another business prior to the one owned in 1968, and were much more likely to have had prior managerial or sales experience. They came from blue-collar working backgrounds much less often, more often had fathers who were white-collar workers, and more often reported that they had close relatives in business.

Whites with relatives in business were generally more successful than blacks with relatives in business, as measured by size of establishment. It is possible that the business relatives of blacks in the sample owned small marginal businesses and, thus, could not offer as much help. However, Caplovitz noted that the black owners were much more likely than the white owners to approve of their children selecting business careers. Those most likely to aspire to entrepreneurship are at early stages of development: While not affluent, they are upwardly mobile. Caplovitz thus concluded that the blacks in this survey were probably at early stages of social mobility, and that this indicated positive future developments in entrepreneurship for blacks.

5. Kent Gilbreath. *Red Capitalism: An Analysis of the Navajo Economy.* **Norman, Okla.: University of Oklahoma Press, 1973.**

• This study synthesized anthropological and sociological information on Navajo traits and analyzed the traits in relation to business development. It identified elements of Navajo culture that have impeded business development in the past. According to this study, attempts to initiate small enterprises on reservations have failed because Navajo entrepreneurs overextend credit to their families and are then unable to collect the debts. Religion has impeded capital accumulation, because it sanctions accusations against the wealthy and because the cost of religious ceremonies is high. Saving is not a widespread habit among the Navajos, thus they seldom accumulate enough personal savings for business investments. Navajos have developed the habit of commuting to towns on the reservation's periphery to shop. "Going to town" has become a pleasurable social affair. This drains-off potential customers for Navajo-owned businesses, which are nearly always on the reservations. Other impediments to Navajo business development are a lack of English fluency, which inhibits their dealings with non-Navajo suppliers and wholesalers, and the absence of a competitive spirit in business matters, perhaps because they have never had a market economy to foster competition.

6a. Andrew Brimmer. "The Negro in the National Economy." In *American Negro Reference Book,* **edited by John David. Englewood Cliffs, N.J.: Prentice-Hall, 1966.**

6b. Andrew Brimmer. "Desegregation and Negro Leadership." In *Business Leadership and the Negro Crisis,* **edited by Eli Ginsberg. New York: McGraw-Hill, 1968.**

• In these two papers, Brimmer argued that not only do segregation and discrimination shape black-owned businesses, but more importantly, that black-owned businesses benefit directly from segregation. According to Brimmer, black businesses existed primarily because whites were reluctant—in some cases simply unwilling—to offer a wide range of the services demanded by blacks. Black businesses therefore enjoy protected markets.

Behind the wall of segregation which cut Negroes off from many public services, there grew up a whole new area of opportunity. Behind this wall of protection emerged the Negro physician, the Negro lawyer, and, above all, the Negro businessman.

This segregated market, serving as a protective tariff, was the foundation for black business communities of personal services, professional services, and public accommodations. In fields where black customers had relatively free access to retail establishments (such as department stores), black-owned firms had typically been nonviable. Thus progress toward desegregation, according to Brimmer, would merely undermine black businesses. The erosion of segregation and discrimination gave blacks greater access to public accommodations, and white firms were increasingly catering to buyers without regard to race. As the tariff wall fell, Brimmer suggested, most black firms would face very hard times. Brimmer concluded that many Negro firms lacked the technical, managerial, and marketing competence needed to compete successfully in the business world.

7. Timothy Bates. "The Potential of Black Capitalism." *Public Policy* **21 (Winter 1973).**   • This study challenged Brimmer's notion that declining segregation and discrimination undermine the black business community. It offered a counter theory of black business development that suggested that the erosion of discrimination would usher in a new era of opportunity for black entrepreneurs.

Brimmer's claim that segregation and discrimination protected black business was a one-sided interpretation of the historical development of black entrepreneurship in America. The protected markets thesis fails to explore causal relationships between segregation and discrimination and the stunted state of the black business community. Among the more important causal relationships is that financial capital sources—such as commercial banks—have frequently been off-limits to black firms. Another is that discrimination in the labor market makes it difficult for blacks to generate the initial equity investment for business formation. The lack of black construction companies in skilled crafts such as plumbing is partially caused by the traditional practice of barring blacks from most apprentice programs in the building trades.

These factors partially explain the black business community's small size and industry orientation. Scarcity of financial capital has caused the overwhelming majority of black firms to concentrate in lines of business requiring little capital. In the surveys of Pierce and Farmer cited above, black entrepreneurs identified their inability to obtain credit as a serious handicap in the competitive struggle for business success. Declines in discrimination lessen key constraints that have historically thwarted black business progress. When capital access constraints ease, black businesses naturally expand into more highly capitalized lines of business in which they formerly had been unable to compete on an equal basis. If capital markets remain open to blacks, then the entire nature of the black business community may shift away from its traditional orientation. Data on blacks receiving loans from the Small Business Administration were offered to support this position. The protected markets thesis does not distinguish between white firms serving white clienteles and those oriented toward black customers. Denying blacks service in most white-owned restaurants does not logically imply that blacks must have patronized black-owned restaurants. They may have chosen to patronize white-owned restaurants that catered to black clienteles. If white entrepreneurs can operate profitably by serving black clienteles, they exploit such opportunities, particularly in highly competitive lines of business requiring little capital investment. Only rarely have deterrents to entry effectively kept white firms from competing with black businesses for the dollars of black consumers. The protected markets thesis, for example, appears to be valid in the case of the life insurance industry, which has more monopolistic characteristics.

8a. Andrew Brimmer and Henry Terrell. "The Economic Potential of Black Capitalism." *Public Policy* 19 (Spring 1971).

8b. Andrew Brimmer. "Small Business and Economic Development in the Negro Community." In *Black Americans and White Business*, edited by Edwin Epstein and David Hampton. Encino, Calif.: Dickinson Publishing, 1971.

• Brimmer and Terrell attempted to document empirically the marginal nature of black business and its reliance on the protected market that segregation provides. In evaluating data describing black-owned businesses, the authors claimed that the general pattern of black entrepreneurship is a mosaic of small, service oriented businesses that owe their existence to a protective barrier of segregation. Utilizing a sample of 564 firms, the authors observed that the most common lines of black business are barber shops and beauty parlors (18.2 percent), groceries (14.5 percent), restaurants (9.6 percent), and laundries (7.1 percent). Mean 1968 sales for these black-owned firms were as follows:

Type of firm	Mean 1968 sales
Laundries	$14,655
Beauty and barber shops	$6,678
Groceries	$28,258
Restaurants	$7,346
All service and retail establishments	$18,065

The 1963 Census of Business reported that the mean gross sales per establishment for all service and retail firms in the United States were $102,538. Finally, Brimmer and Terrell estimated regression equations that suggested that very small black-owned firms are very inefficient.

The authors then estimated the job creation potential of black businesses that were expected to open between 1971 and 1980. They estimated that black firms would create no jobs in the construction, manufacturing, and transportation industries. "This omission was not accidental; rather it resulted from the fact that there are few Negro-owned firms competing in these types of businesses" (pp. 304-6).

Brimmer, in his 1971 article, "Small Business and Economic Development in the Negro Community," presented data describing the low wealth holdings, high levels of installment debt, and generally low incomes typical of black households in 1967. The figures supported his position that firms catering to black clienteles serve markets that are weak due to deficient purchasing power. Brimmer indicated that if a firm's target market is the black community, the least promising lines are the larger scale businesses such as manufacturing, construction, and wholesaling. The limited market in the black community denies such firms "the economies of scale that are a precondition of long-run economic development" (p. 270). Small business ownership, according to Brimmer, does "offer modest opportunities for some potential Negro entrepreneurs" (p. 270), particularly if they seek either racially diverse clienteles or largely nonminority clienteles. Opportunities are better in the national economy, because the greater purchasing power that can be tapped allows firms to expand in size and scope.

9. Timothy Bates.
Black Capitalism: A Quantitative Analysis.
New York: Praeger, 1973.

• This study re-analyzed the data for the 564 black-owned firms evaluated by Brimmer and Terrell in the study reviewed above and found indications that their computations were incorrect. As with many surveys, nonresponse was a major problem. For example, in Durham, North Carolina, students of a sociology class interviewed 80 black business owners, but only 18 of them would reveal their sales and profits figures. Brimmer and Terrell assumed that all nonresponders had zero sales and profits. They did not distinguish between those who actually had zero sales and profits and those who had sales and profits but chose not to reveal them.

In this study, Bates argued that the Brimmer and Terrell analysis had a more fundamental problem: it assumed that the black firms emerging in the 1970s would be replicas of the existing species; it did not consider the possibility of evolution and progress. Data from the Small Business Administration (SBA) suggest that it is invalid to assume that new and expanding black firms will conform to the stereotype of the small, undercapitalized, inefficient firm of the past. To determine the "potential" of black entrepreneurship, one must examine data on existing firms that are expanding and new firms that are being formed. One cannot simply examine a cross-section of the black business community and extrapolate the status quo into the future.

SBA and banking industry programs in fact expanded the financing available to black firms, particularly after Project OWN was introduced in 1968. Under Project OWN, the SBA insured long-term bank loans to minority firms against default risk. Bates then analyzed a sample of 559 black firms that received SBA guaranteed bank loans and direct loans between 1967 and 1970—precisely the period in which capital market access increased substantially for black entrepreneurs. The key issue that is empirically analyzed is this: how did black businesses respond when government programs suddenly increased substantially the availability of business loans? The findings indicate that many of the firms that were created or expanded with the help of SBA loans were in nontraditional lines of black enterprise such as wholesaling, manufacturing, contracting services, and types of retailing—furniture, appliances, apparel—that require considerable investment in inventory. Bates concluded that increased access to financial capital enabled many black entrepreneurs to break away from the traditional lines of small, labor intensive, service oriented business enterprises.

Editorial note: The analysis and policy recommendations in the Bates and Brimmer studies differ mainly in terms of emphasis: they are not diametrically opposed. Note that Bates' criticisms of Brimmer's theoretical and empirical work do not necessarily contradict the protected market thesis. Rather, the key point is that one must consider the changing nature of all of the major forces shaping the black business community, not merely the trend toward desegregation in the marketplace for consumer goods and services, before making predictions about the potential of black entrepreneurship. At the policy level,

Brimmer called for full participation in an integrated national economy: "This holds for Negroes who want to be businessmen as well as for everyone else" (Brimmer 1971a, p.270; see no. 8b). Similarly, Bates has stated that "the prospects for progress in the black business realm appear to be minimal for the ghetto-oriented firms. . . firms that are increasingly competing in the broader marketplace, however, are likely to continue to expand and diversify" (Bates1989a, p.27; see no. 71).

10. Timothy Bates. "An Econometric Analysis of Lending to Black Businessmen." *The Review of Economics and Statistics* **55 (August 1973).**

• This analysis of black and white firms that received SBA loans sought to distinguish between firms that were successfully repaying their loans and firms whose loans were seriously delinquent or in liquidation. The findings indicated that the evaluation criteria that are most appropriate for judging the credit risks of white borrowers do not effectively judge credit risk among black borrowers.

Influential black businessmen have asserted that loan officials incorrectly analyze loan applications from blacks, because they fail to recognize that black entrepreneurs can subsist at substantially lower income levels than their white counterparts and still repay their loans. The statistical findings of this study strongly supported this notion, and the failure of loan officers to recognize this fact generates underfunding of the loan requests of black business borrowers.

One oddity of the SBA loan programs is that the larger black firms received relatively smaller loans than the smallest firms. This lending pattern is rooted in the two very different SBA programs that were funding black enterprise. (This is discussed in Bates 1975; see no. 14). Among the loan recipients analyzed in this study, mean total business assets (pre-loan) were $34,652 and mean loan size was $28,220. Yet, the mean loan-to-assets ratio was 189 percent, reflecting the tendency of small firms to receive loan amounts far in excess of their total business assets. When the same loan recipients are divided into two groups consisting of (1) borrowers who were current in repaying their loans and (2) borrowers who were delinquent, the mean values were as follows:

	Current borrowers	Delinquent borrowers
Total assets prior to loan approval	$48,524	$19,740
Loan amount, as a percentage of total assets	159%	219%

Discriminant analysis was applied first to black business loan recipients and then to white recipients to identify the factors that most effectively differentiate between current and delinquent borrowers for both blacks and whites. For the black borrowers, firm size—as measured by total assets—most effectively differentiated current from delinquent loan recipients. Among white borrowers, business net worth differentiated current from delinquent loans. Among black firms, net worth measures had no power whatsoever in distinguishing between those who met their loan payments and those who were delinquent. Several factors were similar for whites and blacks: firms current on their loans tended to have good credit ratings and balance sheet liquidity, and their owners had managerial experience.

Discriminant analysis was also used to analyze owners receiving loans to finance business start-ups. Among blacks forming new firms, total personal income prior to entering self-employment was the strongest single predictor of loan repayment: those with higher personal incomes were current in repaying their loans. Among whites, the factors most strongly associated with timely reparyment of loans were good credit ratings and prior management experience.

11. Robert Browne. "Cash Flows in a Ghetto Economy." *The Review of Black Political Economy* 1 (Spring 1971).

• Proponents of economic development in ghettos have emphasized the role that cash flow plays in exacerbating inner-city economic underdevelopment. Brown argues that money too often passes through the urban ghetto without lingering long enough to turn over several times and thereby generate incomes for community residents. In addition, ghetto residents often do their shopping at stores located elsewhere; when they do shop locally, they frequently patronize stores owned by outsiders. Internal income flows that might support greater economic activity within the ghetto are largely absent. If neighborhood businesses were owned by local residents who spent their incomes within the ghetto, more money would recirculate within the black community and the multiplier effects would, of course, tend to be greater. Browne therefore advocated developing black-owned businesses as a strategy for slowing the speed with which money flows out of ghetto communities.

Browne's argument was reinforced by a study of Hough, a depressed ghetto neighborhood in Cleveland. The study was published in 1971, shortly after Browne's article appeared. Based on household spending diaries, the Hough study documented the outflow of income in ordinary household spending. It showed that the marginal propensity to spend in Hough was only 0.13. That is, for each additional dollar of family expenditures, only thirteen cents was spent within Hough (Oakland, Sparrow, and Stettler 1971).

12. Don Markwalder. "The Potential for Black Business." *The Review of Black Political Economy* **11 (Spring 1981).**

• Andrew Brimmer was right, argued Markwalder; the potential of "black capitalism" is very limited. Sales of black-owned businesses increased in real (i.e., inflation-adjusted) terms by less than 2 percent between 1972 and 1977. This compared with an increase in the real GNP of 14.4 percent over this same period. Thus, according to Markwalder, the controversy between Bates and Brimmer was settled: "black business does not appear to have the potential that Bates once envisioned" (p. 311). Blacks cannot hold their own in the world of small business because they lack the wealth, education, business experience, or political clout required.

13. Timothy Bates. "The Potential for Black Business: A Comment." *The Review of Black Political Economy* **12 (Winter 1983).**

• This was a critique of Markwalder's 1981 article (no. 12). It showed that two divergent trends typified black business development in the 1970s: (1) many traditional lines of black enterprise, such as barber shops and mom and pop grocery stores, declined and (2) many emerging fields showed progress.

Markwalder's error lay in using overly aggregated data, which caused him to conclude that slow growth—and not two divergent trends—typifies black entrepreneurship. Between 1972 and 1977, the proportion of black firms operating in the traditional food and personal service industries shrank from 32.5 percent to 28.1 percent. During this same time period, in contrast, the number of black firms in the emerging business services field grew by over 50 percent, and the number of employees in this industry group increased 56.8 percent (from 11,800 to 18,502 jobs).

In some industries black self-employment is indeed growing slowly, but the reality in many fields is one of two extremes—either rapid growth or outright decline. Aggregate statistics incorrectly suggest a picture of slow growth. The reality is a major recompositioning—a qualitative restructuring—of the very nature of the black business community. The more numerous traditional lines of black enterprise are in a state of decline, whereas the skill- and capital-intensive fields are expanding. The trajectory of black entrepreneurship is being determined in the long run by the performance of this latter group of firms.

Government Programs to Assist Minority Businesses

Three types of minority business assistance programs have attracted the attention of researchers. The loan programs launched by the Small Business Administration (SBA) in the late 1960s have been studied most extensively, whereas the Minority Enterprise Small Business Investment Company (MESBIC) programs have been a secondary focus. In the 1980s, research interest shifted to the various minority business procurement and set-aside programs offered by federal, state, and local governments.

A word of caution is in order as one reviews the studies of SBA and MESBIC loan programs: all of the data analyzed in the studies are at least 10 years old. Criticisms of the MESBIC programs, in particular, may be dated in light of the growth and maturity that typified many of the programs in the 1980s. In response to charges of program ineffectiveness—often based on the studies described in this section––the SBA has become quite protective of internal information on the effectiveness of its programs. This, of course, has made it difficult to analyze recent trends in the impact of SBA activities on the state of the minority business community.

18

Among the studies reviewed in this section, those by Bates (nos. 14, 15, and 18) and Richard Klein (no. 17) describe the nature of the SBA minority business loan programs, focusing particularly on loan terms and borrower default rates. Douglas Johnson (no. 19) criticized the SBA for lending disproportionately to the types of small firms that are most apt to provide low-wage, unstable jobs. Bates and William Bradford (no. 20) documented the general decline in the number of loans extended to minority businesses under the SBA programs in the mid-1970s. John Dominguez (no. 16) provided an overview of the MESBIC program, and Alfred Osborne and Michael Granfield (no. 22d) focused on the operation of a specific California MESBIC.

The studies of minority business procurement programs summarized in this section approached the topic from three perspectives. The two government studies (nos. 21a and 21b) were highly critical of the SBA's 8(a) procurement program. In contrast, the evaluations of the Local Public Works Program (nos. 23a and 23b), an ambitious minority business set-aside effort run by the Department of Transportation, were generally favorable. Finally, two Bates studies examined data on over a thousand minority firms that were actual or potential participants in corporate as well as government minority business procurement and set-aside programs.

14. Timothy Bates. "Government as Financial Intermediary for Minority Entrepreneurs." *The Journal of Business* **48 (October 1975).**

• Programs that provide minority entrepreneurs access to long-term credit on preferential terms have made a considerable impact on the size and scope of black businesses. Nevertheless, although the programs appear to be broadening the industry composition of the black business community, they are also producing high rates of loan default and business failure. The inherent strengths and weaknesses of the SBA's loan programs can best be understood by examining their conception and administration.

In terms of the numbers of businesses assisted, the largest SBA program has been the Economic Opportunity Loan (EOL) program. It was designed to help low-income entrepreneurs who operate tiny, generally nonviable firms. Minority entrepreneurs who have the requisite qualities associated with business success—education, skills, financial capital, and the like—are ineligible for EOLs. Thus, the EOL program produced a high incidence of loan default, but this was perfectly consistent with its underlying ideology.

In terms of dollar volume, the largest SBA loan program has been the one designated 7(a), which consists largely of bank loans guaranteed against default by the SBA. The EOL and 7(a) loan programs are available to nonminorities as well as minorities, although the latter are given more favorable terms. The 7(a) program has enabled thousands of minority firms to establish banking ties. Unlike the EOL effort, the 7(a) program targets larger and more promising minority firms.

Prior to 1968, virtually all SBA loans to minority borrowers were EOLs. In the five fiscal years 1969-1973, 24,422 of the 36,782 SBA loans to minorities were EOLs. In 1973, the average SBA loan amount to minority borrowers was $19,795 under the EOL program and $61,157 under all other programs. Mean SBA loan amount to all nonminority borrowers in 1973 exceeded $100,000.

The state of the EOL program in the early 1970s was paradoxical: the strongest loan recipients most frequently succeeded in business but they came from high-income groups and, therefore, were not technically eligible for the program. The truly disadvantaged loan recipients failed in droves. Altering the EOL lending philosophy and refusing to lend to minority businesses in the absence of reasonable prospects for repayment would cut the SBA's delinquency and default rates.

Editorial note: Those who repay their loans successfully are identified in Bates 1973b; see no. 10 above.

15. Timothy Bates. "Financing Black Enterprises." *The Journal of Finance* 29 (June 1974).

• SBA loans extended to minority-owned firms under direct loan programs and bank loan guarantee programs became a major source of funds for tens of thousands of firms in the late 1960s and the 1970s. Earlier studies (such as Bates 1973b; see no. 10) noted the tendency to fund the smaller minority firms most generously. This study explored in detail the types of firms that receive the larger (and smaller) loans under the applicable SBA, EOL, and 7(a) loan programs. The SBA states that loans to minorities "are processed under relaxed eligibility criteria with emphasis on the applicant's character and ability to repay the loan and other obligations from the profits of the business" (Small Business Administration 1971, p. 13).

This comparative study of the loan amounts extended under SBA programs in the 1967-1970 time period indicates that black-owned firms indeed received larger loans, on average, than white-owned firms. Applicable mean values were as follows:

	Blacks	Whites
Loan size	$28,220	$25,169
Loan size divided by total assets of the firm (pre-loan)	1.89	0.97

Linear regression models indicated that the SBA is concerned largely with business cash flow and collateral when it approves loan amounts. Per dollar of business cash flow, the black owner—other factors constant—receives an incremental 0.96 loan dollars, versus 0.29 loan dollars for whites. Regarding collateral, both blacks and whites receive an incremental 0.36 loan dollars for each collateral dollar. The findings indicated further that the SBA is not afraid to increase leverage to fairly high levels: firms having little net worth often receive large loans, whether the borrower is black or white. Holding loan amount constant, the SBA extends another relative advantage to black borrowers by approving longer loan maturities for them than for white borrowers.

Factors associated with long-run business viability and loan repayment ability—particularly firm credit rating and owner managerial experience—are largely ignored when loan amounts are determined. Particularly among black borrowers, cash flow is the key to determining loan amounts: the emphasis is on granting larger loans to firms most likely to meet payment obligations in the short run. One odd aspect with this emphasis on short-term repayment capability is the fact that the loans are all long-term, frequently carrying maturities exceeding five years. If one goal is to minimize loan delinquency and default in the long run, then the SBA is focusing on inappropriate factors when it approves loan amounts for black-owned firms.

16. John Dominguez.
Capital Flows in Minority Areas. **Lexington, Mass.: Lexington Books, 1976.**

• Another SBA-connected program, the Minority Enterprise Small Business Investment Company (MESBIC) project, has been something of a fiasco. This project was launched by the Office of Minority Business Enterprise in conjunction with the SBA. As privately owned, privately managed venture capital corporations, MESBICs are supposed to furnish four services to minority-owned firms. One, they provide venture capital by purchasing an equity interest in the business. Two, they provide long-term capital by lending funds (normally subordinate to other creditors) to the business, often with warrants permitting MESBICs to purchase an equity position. Three, they guarantee loans made by third parties. And four, they provide general management and technical assistance.

Congress has given MESBICs the power to leverage their privately invested capital by selling long-term debentures and preferred stock to the SBA. For example, if they have $500,000 or more of capital and capital surplus, they may sell up to three times this sum in debentures to the SBA, priced at the cost of capital to the government (the rate of interest that the U.S. treasury is paying to holders of Treasury bonds and bills).

The MESBICs described by Dominguez were in trouble. Their most severe problems were undercapitalization and weak cash flow. These may simply have been symptoms, however, of a more fundamental malaise: most were not able to cope successfully with the risks of financing small minority businesses. MESBICs often generate negative cash flows because of the extended periods before equity investments start to yield dividends. To cope with cash flow crises, they often avoid equity investments and turn, increasingly, to granting loans to minority firms. They fail, therefore, to provide the equity capital that is essential for minority business development. MESBIC clients are certainly not riskless, and the steady demands that loan repayments place on cash flow predictably push some of the firms into default. When loan losses occur, MESBICs acquire capital-base erosion problems on top of their cash flow difficulties. Virtually all successful SBA small business investment companies were initially capitalized at $1 million or more, and they invested their funds in larger small businesses. Few MESBICs are capitalized at this level. Facing investment losses, interest payments on borrowed funds, and operating expenses, MESBICs often quickly erode their inadequate capital resources. Among the 67 MESBICs that Dominguez studied, less than one-third of the available funds were invested in minority businesses. Over 60 percent of the resources were held in risk-free liquid assets such as bank certificates of deposit, which paid rates of return exceeding the MESBIC cost of funds from their government borrowings. Hence, in many instances, they have been engaging in riskless arbitrage operations whereby the SBA lends them money at a rate equal to the cost of funds to the federal treasury and they invest these funds in higher yielding yet very safe securities. While the minority community suffers from a severe lack of venture capital, MESBIC funds languish in bank certificates of deposit.

17. Richard Klein. "SBA's Business Loan Programs." Atlanta Economic Review 23 (September/October 1978).

• Klein's estimates of the failure rates among small businesses borrowing through the SBA's loan programs during 1969-1971 were as follows:

- nonminority 7(a) failure rate: 15.7 percent
- nonminority EOL failure rate: 27.8 percent
- minority 7(a) failure rate: 24.6 percent
- minority EOL failure rate: 49.7 percent.

Editorial note: The EOL and 7(a) programs were described in "Government as Financial Intermediary for Minority Entrepreneurs," (no. 14) reviewed above.

18. Timothy Bates. "Small Business Administration Loan Programs." In Sources of Financing for Small Business, edited by Paul Horvitz and R. Richardson Pettit. Greenwich, Conn.: JAI Press, 1983.

• It is difficult to determine what the SBA is accomplishing via its minority lending efforts. The SBA relies exclusively on the number of loans being approved to measure the success of its programs. However, loan approval statistics are very crude measures of lending effectiveness. This study used an alternative figure—the number of successful minority and nonminority businesses assisted through the 7(a) and EOL loan programs—to measure the SBA's impact upon small business. Firms were classified as "successful" if they repay their loans.

Although the SBA claims that it has approved in excess of 30,000 loans annually, the number of firms actually assisted is considerably less due to nondisbursal of approved loans and the use of new loans to refinance previous SBA loans. Among samples of firms that actually received loans, estimated failure rates range from a low of 15.7 percent for nonminority businesses receiving 7(a) loans to a high of 53.3 percent for minority businesses receiving EOL loans. In conjunction with nondisbursals and refundings, the failure rates bring the proportion of successful firms assisted down to less than 60 percent of all SBA loan approvals. Because of their high failure rates, successful EOL loan recipients account for less than 50 percent of all EOL net loan disbursals, whereas slightly over 78 percent of the 7(a) loan recipients are estimated to translate eventually into businesses that repay their loans. The higher observed rates of failure among minority borrowers are rooted largely in their disproportionately heavy participation in the EOL loan program.

Congressional oversight of SBA loan programs would be greatly facilitated if more comprehensive data on the performance of loan recipients was provided. On key issues such as judging the value of loan programs, complete and accurate data on success and failure rates are essential. Annual breakdowns of the numbers of loan recipients and the proportions of successful firms should be published.

Editorial note: This study was also published under the title, "A Review of the Small Business Administration's Major Loan Programs," in Studies of Small Business Finance: A Report to Congress *(Interagency Task Force on Small Business, 1982). An abbreviated version also appeared in* The Review of Black Political Economy *(Spring 1981).*

19. Douglas Johnson. "Urban Impact Analysis of the Small Business Administration 7(a) and Economic Opportunity Loan Programs." MIT Urban and Community Impacts Discussion Paper No. 7 (1980).

• Johnson argued that the SBA should concentrate its lending among substantive firms such as manufacturers that offer both better wages and more stable working conditions, relative to the more common small service and retail establishment firms. The distribution of EOL loans across industry groupings reveals a stronger emphasis, relative to the 7(a) program, on lending to retail and service establishments; loans to manufacturing and wholesaling are less frequent. Among minority borrowers, retail and service firms received over 73 percent of the EOL loans approved in the 1975-78 period. Minority wholesaling and manufacturing firms accounted for 11.3 percent of EOL loans. These two industry groups received 16.1 percent of the 7(a) loans in this time period. On a closely related point, Klein (no. 17 above) asserted that "much of the SBA's financial assistance has been channeled on a de facto basis to companies in industries where additional competition may be considered undesirable and where SBA's financial assistance may even cause detrimental effects" (p. 36). Creating additional firms in traditionally crowded lines of business leads, in many instances, to a destructive zero sum game in which new firms financed by the SBA succeed only by driving existing entrepreneurs into bankruptcy.

20. Timothy Bates and William Bradford. *Financing Black Economic Development.* **New York: Academic Press, 1979. (Chapters 8 and 9.)**

• High loan delinquency and default rates among black borrowers have been instrumental in eroding the credibility of government programs designed to finance black-owned businesses. This study indicated that the SBA's EOL program has produced very high default rates primarily because of its underlying philosophy, which requires that its black loan recipients be poor credit risks. The lack of growth since 1972 in SBA loan approvals to minority borrowers is largely accounted for by sharp cutbacks in EOL loans. The number of EOL loan approvals to minority borrowers declined steadily from a peak of 5,791 in 1972 to 2,551 in 1976. The SBA's cutback has therefore been concentrated in the loan program that has produced the highest incidence of delinquency and default among black business borrowers. The availability of EOL loans at low interest rates encouraged many blacks to enter businesses that were nonviable. The resulting sequence of events—failing in business and defaulting on loan obligations—placed severe hardships on many unsuccessful entrepreneurs. By reducing the number of EOL loans, the SBA may be financing the creation and perpetuation of fewer marginally viable and nonviable black-owned firms.

Editorial note: The EOL program was abolished in the early 1980s.

21a. Small Business Administration 8(a) Review Board. *Report and Recommendations on the Section 8(a) Program for A. Vernon Weaver, Administrator.* **Washington, D.C.: Small Business Administration, 1978.**

21b. Comptroller General of the United States. *The SBA 8(a) Program: A Promise Unfulfilled.* **Washington, D.C.: General Accounting Office, 1981.**

• After the 1967 amendment to the Economic Opportunity Act was enacted, the SBA established a new program, under section 8(a), that expressly directed federal contracts to firms owned by disadvantaged businessmen. The dollar amount of section 8(a) procurement contracts—amounting to a modest $8.9 million in 1969—grew to $208 million in 1973 and to $768 million in 1978.

Although the SBA is not required to award 8(a) contracts exclusively to minorities, it has largely operated as a minority set-aside program. This report of the 8(a) review board indicated that 96 percent of the 8(a) companies were owned by members of minority groups. Entry into the 8(a) program is contingent upon SBA approval of the business plan prepared by prospective firms. The business plan identifies the types of assistance needed to create a profitable, self-sustaining business. It projects the amount of 8(a) contract support needed for the firm to reach self-sufficiency as well as the firm's operating performance for the next three years. The criteria used by SBA to accept or reject 8(a) business applicants have been vague and inconsistent through time.

The 8(a) approach to business assistance has generally been unsuccessful. In theory, 8(a) firms use their contract support to attain self-sufficiency and then they "graduate" from the program. In fact, graduation is rare (five firms graduated during the 1975-80 time period), and a handful of politically well-connected firms have gotten the bulk of the contracts. According to the 1981 report by the General Accounting Office, only 166 of the 4,598 firms that had ever participated in the 8(a) program graduated as competitive businesses. Many 8(a) firms have had all of the help that the SBA has to offer, but they still have not developed into competitive firms. The 8(a) program is designed to assist the marginal entrepreneur as opposed to the successful or promising self-employed minority businessperson. Government programs that are designed to aid the less-promising minority entrepreneurs have consistently been ineffective, and the 8(a) program is no exception.

22a. William Tabb. "Viewing Minority Economic Development as a Problem in Political Economy." *American Economic Review* **62 (May 1972).**

22b. William Tabb. "What Ever Happened to Black Economic Development?" *The Review of Black Political Economy* **9 (Summer 1979).**

22c. Alfred Osborne. "The Welfare Effects of Black Capitalists on the Black Community." *The Review of Black Political Economy* **6 (Summer 1976).**

22d. Alfred Osborne and Michael Granfield. "The Potential of Black Capitalism in Perspective." *Public Policy* **24 (Fall 1976).**

• These four articles are typical of the social sciences literature that has been critical of the notion that government should assist minority-owned firms. A recurring theme in these articles is that minority-owned firms—being few in number and small in size and scope—are collectively insignificant. Cross-sectional data were cited to demonstrate that minority enterprises are heavily concentrated in several lines of small-scale service and retailing activity that hold minimal potential for growth.

Osborne argued that the total income of blacks often drops when they move from wage and salary employment to self-employment. Osborne and Granfield used a sample of 45 firms in California to demonstrate that government subsidized funds are used inefficiently by minority enterprises.

Tabb, whose broader political and economic concerns transcend the details of government programs, contended that minority business promotion efforts divert attention from the more fundamental problems facing minority groups. The scholarly positions of these authors are quite complementary since the demonstrated failure of existing governmental promotion efforts certainly supports the notion that minority business programs are not addressing the basic problems that too many minorities face, such as inadequate educational and training opportunities and limited access to decent jobs.

Editorial note: Tabb, Osborne, and Granfield raised important issues that are addressed in detail in Part 2 of this bibliography. In a study by Bates not discussed in this volume (Bates 1978), the appropriateness of the computations appearing in the Osborne and Granfield article is challenged: The evidence does not indicate inefficient use of government subsidized funds.

23a. U.S. Department of Commerce, Economic Development Administration. *Local Public Works Program: Final Report*. Washington, D.C.: U.S. Department of Commerce, 1980.

23b. The Granville Corporation. "A Longitudinal Analysis of Minority Business Enterprises Participating in the Local Public Works Program." Unpublished report to the Economic Development Administration (December 1982).

• One problem with minority business set-asides has been that the government incurs higher procurement costs as a result of using firms that are less experienced relative to nonminority firms. Higher procurement costs are inherent in set-asides such as the 8(a) program, which assumes that the contract recipients are not competitive. In the procurement programs that seek to utilize the most efficient minority firms available, however, higher procurement costs are generally a transitory phenomenon and they are not necessarily wasteful in the long run.

Consider, for example, the widely studied 1977 Local Public Works Employment Act, which contained a large minority business set-aside provision. Approximately 18 percent of the expenditures under this act accrued to minority firms, and this resulted in an estimated overall cost increase of over one percent in the construction programs that were ultimately completed. In the absence of minority participation, not only could the construction have taken place at a cost saving of over one percent but certain projects could have been completed faster.

The construction industry is traditionally one in which general contractors work with a closely knit group of subcontractors. This old-boy network allows subcontractors to maximize their chances of receiving business from general contractors. This network is exactly what shut out minority firms—few of which are large enough to be general contractors—from their fair share of large-scale construction projects. The 1977 Local Public Works Employment Act changed this state of affairs by forcing general contractors to subcontract work to minorities. Thus, general contractors had to get to know the minority firms, and the process of opening the lines of communication between general contractors and minority construction firms was not altogether a smooth one.

The process of finding suitable minority subcontractors was, of course, complicated by the uncertainty that general contractors felt in dealing with unknown firms as opposed to dealing with firms from the old-boy network. The key point, though, is that the lines of communication that are opened through this process—although difficult the first time around—promote more competition in construction, which may actually reduce construction costs in the long run. According to Granville's evaluation of the Local Public Works Employment Act, 61 percent of the minority subcontractors continued to do business with the general contractors after their initial Local Public Works Employment contracts were completed. Furthermore, the Local Public Works Employment Act set-aside helped participating minority firms increase their bonding capacity, thus improving their ability to compete for larger scale construction jobs in the future. Breaking down traditional barriers to minority business participation in the economy is not a costless process, but achieving this goal is precisely the intent of minority business set-asides.

24a. Timothy Bates. "Minority Business Set-Asides: Theory and Practice." In *Affirmative Action in Employment and Minority Business Set-Asides*. U.S. Commission on Civil Rights. Washington, D.C.: Government Printing Office, 1985.

24b. Timothy Bates. "Impact of Preferential Procurement Policies on Minority-Owned Businesses." *The Review of Black Political Economy* 14 (Summer 1985).

• Minority business set-aside programs have aided in the creation and expansion of thousands of larger scale minority enterprises in nontraditional fields such as wholesaling, general construction, business services, and large-scale manufacturing. Federal government programs have been emulated by corporations as well as state and local government units. Over the 1970s, the average incomes of minority entrepreneurs expanded much more rapidly than those of self-employed nonminorities. Younger and better-educated minorities have been lured into self-employment by the expanded opportunities in corporate and government markets.

These studies used data on over 1,000 minority firms (as well as a comparison group of nonminority firms) that were drawn from the Dun's Financial Profiles (DFP) data base. Because the firms studied were actual or potential participants in corporate and government minority business procurement and set-aside programs, they were much larger than the mean firm in the minority business universe. For this reason, the sample firms were overrepresented in construction, manufacturing, and wholesaling, relative to all minority businesses. Within the service industry, most of the firms in the sample were in business services, professional services, finance, insurance, and real estate; few of the firms were in personal services and repair services.

Minority business set-aside efforts have been criticized for assisting the larger scale, more profitable minority enterprises. Data in these studies showed that the types of firms that participate most actively in minority set-asides are indeed much larger and more profitable than the average firm in the minority business universe. But the data also showed that these minority-owned firms lag behind their nonminority counterparts in important respects. In comparison to nonminority firms they are less profitable as a group; their incidence of nonprofitability is more than four times greater; they are very highly leveraged and thus vulnerable to delinquency on debt obligations (and hence actual failure); and they are younger.

On balance, the large-scale minority businesses in the DFP sample analyzed in these studies did have unique problems, particularly in the realm of leverage, but the evidence indicates that both minority and nonminority firms become less highly leveraged as they grow older. In addition, for minorities, firm age is directly related to dollar levels of firm size and profits. As the age distribution of minority firms begins to approach that of nonminority firms, their leverage problems should begin to lessen and their aggregate profits should begin to rise.

Under many types of set-aside programs mandated by legislation, such as the 1977 Local Public Works Employment Act, minority enterprises are selected on the basis of merit. In that respect, these programs are fundamentally different from 8(a) contracts, which are awarded on the basis of need. Under the non-8(a) type programs, even though nonminorities are shut out, the minority firms must compete with other minority firms. Thus, these programs provide minority enterprises with only partial protection from competition in the awarding of procurement contracts. A federal agency that purchases goods or services from a minority vendor will—other things being constant—pick the low-cost supplier over high-cost alternatives, and similarly will favor the vendor that produces reliably over the one that produces haphazardly. Over time, therefore, procurement business will flow increasingly to the most efficient minority enterprises. Unlike with the 8(a) contracts, the forces of marketplace competition will be operative: agencies will strive to minimize their procurement costs, and in the resulting competitive struggle for procurement contracts the efficient minority business will prosper.

Minority business set-aside programs that demand efficient business performance are the ones that are most useful to society. They are also consistent with the goal of utilizing minority business expansion as a tool for promoting economic development. By encouraging expansion of the more efficient minority enterprises, government is creating the role models and success stories that are vital to the minority business development effort.

25. Timothy Bates. "Black Entrepreneurship and Government Programs." *Journal of Contemporary Studies* 4 (Fall 1981).
• This article is an overview of many of the themes discussed in the other studies in this section. It reviewed the widely differing and sometimes inconsistent goals that serve as justifications for minority business assistance programs. The most fundamental conflict in goals concerns the question of who the target recipients should be—the most deprived minorities who for that reason need help the most, or those who need help less but have much better prospects for business success. Looking at the contrasts in potential beneficiaries highlights contrasting objectives: whether to use aid as a kind of poverty program to redistribute wealth to poor self-employed minorities or whether to create strong firms capable of generating jobs for underemployed ghetto residents and which will encourage success stories and role models.

Loan and procurement programs in the 1970s were often radically misdirected: promising minority firms were frequently ineligible for loans and procurement contracts, whereas those who were eligible failed in droves. This study reviewed the evidence of failure in the EOL and 8(a) programs and recommended abandoning the objective of targeting those who are least capable of succeeding in business. In contrast, the SBA 7(a) loan program has improved capital market access for a more promising group of firms. Recipients of these loans have created and expanded thousands of larger scale minority-owned businesses in emerging fields such as business services, manufacturing, and wholesaling. For procurement assistance to serve as a viable program for minority business assistance, it must seek to assist the stronger, more capable minority-owned firms.

Modern Quantitative Studies

Minority-Owned Businesses

Traditionally, the typical firm in the minority business community has been the mom and pop food store, the beauty parlor, the barbershop. These tiny firms, when owned by blacks and Hispanics, are concentrated in minority residential areas and serve local clienteles. Over the past 20 years, they have been in a state of continuous decline, particularly the black-owned firms, less so the Asian-owned ones.

The growth sector is dominated today by larger scale firms that most likely serve racially diverse clienteles. Increasingly, they sell to other businesses, including large corporations and units of government. They are commonly run by entrepreneurs who have attended college. This is particularly true in the rapid growth areas, which include the skill-intensive service industries: finance, business services, and professional services. In the construction industry, the growth sector has also consisted of larger firms that do not rely primarily on minority clienteles. Opportunities offered by special corporate and government procurement programs targeted to minority businesses have contributed heavily to the growth of these emerging lines of minority-owned business.

Recent studies of small business dynamics indicate that all minority groups—blacks, Asians, and Hispanics—tend to prosper in self-employment in direct proportion to the degree that they are moving away from traditional fields such as personal services. The evolution away from traditional industries and into emerging lines of business over the past three decades has been possible because business owners have substantially increased their education and skill levels as well as their financial investments in their enterprises.

Trends in the present-day community of black businesses can be explained largely in terms of the following traditional-emerging business duality: *traditional firms* tend to be small-scale, have high failure rates, and generate few jobs, because their owners have minimal levels of education and skill and invest small amounts of financial capital in their businesses; whereas *emerging firms* are most commonly started by better educated blacks (many of whom have attended four or more years of college) whose financial capital investments are high relative to the investments of blacks in traditional lines of business. For these very reasons—that the owners are highly competent and make larger financial investments—the emerging firms tend to be larger, have lower failure rates, and generate more jobs relative to their traditional cohorts.

Since the 1960s, the minority business community has clearly started to diversify and expand in response to an influx of entrepreneurial talent and financial capital. Aggregate figures on minority-owned business understate this progress because they fail to identify two divergent trends: the absolute decline in many traditional lines of business, and the real progress in the emerging fields. This conclusion was reached by Bates (nos. 26 and 29) and by Robert Suggs (no. 28). The studies by Frank Fratoe and Ronald Meeks (no. 27) and by Peter Bearse (no. 30) focused on the low rate of entry into self-employment typical of blacks and Hispanics. Richard Stevens (no. 31) argued that the lower growth rates of the black business community and the higher growth rates among Asians reflect, most directly, their respective low (black) and high (Asian) rates of new business formation; Hispanics lie between these two extremes. Finally, Fratoe (no. 32) compiled several measures of social capital (i.e., social resources available from group support networks such as kinship and community support groups) that, he asserted, help explain the various rates of self-employment observed among minority groups.

26. Timothy Bates. "Self-Employed Minorities: Traits and Trends." *Social Science Quarterly* 68 (September 1987).

• Cross-sectional statistics focusing on one particular point in time invariably highlight the laggard position of self-employed minorities relative to their white counterparts. A more insightful line of research entails examining comparable data at different points in time to trace the changing nature of the minority entrepreneur universe. To trace trends over time, this study examined 1960, 1970, and 1980 census data on self-employed minorities (and nonminorities).

One of the greatest changes in the minority entrepreneur universe has been the industrial diversification. As the table on the next page shows, two lines of business—personal services and retailing—accounted for well over half of all minority enterprises in 1960. Smaller concentrations of minorities were working in other services and in construction. Collectively, these four most common fields—personal services, retail, construction, and other services—accounted for 81.3 percent of the self-employed minorities in 1960. Between 1960 and 1980, however, all of the growth in relative self-employment shares—as measured by the proportions of minority entrepreneurs in various lines of business—took place *outside* of these four lines of minority enterprise (see the table below). Minority self-employment growth was most rapid in four fields that collectively more than doubled their relative share of the entrepreneur pool:

1. business services,
2. finance, insurance, and real estate (FIRE),
3. transportation and communication, and
4. wholesale.

This pattern of stagnation in the traditional lines of minority business and rapid growth in the emerging fields such as business services is a recurring theme that is discussed in other recent studies of minority entrepreneurship.

Industry groups that are growing rapidly are attracting younger, better educated minorities. Fields that have been particularly noteworthy in attracting highly educated minorities include the skill-intensive services and wholesaling. Those who are working in the emerging lines of business have higher earnings than other self-employed minorities and higher earnings than wage and salary workers.

Two industries—personal services and FIRE—illustrate important trends in minority self-employment. Among all minority entrepreneurs in the FIRE industry, 68 percent had attended college (vs. 33 percent for all self-employed minorities), and the majority of the college students had graduated from four-year colleges and universities. Only 5.8 percent of the self-employed minorities working in personal services had graduated from college. With its below average returns to self-employment, personal services offers few opportunities for the highly educated potential entrepreneur; the industry is in a state of long-run decline. FIRE, in contrast, offers above average returns to self-employment, and the minority presence in this industry is growing

Trends in the Relative Incidence of Self-Employed Minorities, by Industry Group, 1960 to 1980

Industry*	Percent of all self-employed minorities in the industry (1960)	(1980)	Percent change since 1960	Growth rate**
Construction	16.7%	16.5%	-1.2%	Stagnant
Manufacturing	4.1	6.0	46.3	Moderate
Transportation, communications, and utilities	3.9	6.0	53.8	Rapid
Wholesale	1.7	3.6	111.8	Rapid
Retail	25.4	25.4	0.0	Stagnant
FIRE	1.4	4.0	185.7	Rapid
Business services	2.4	6.6	175.0	Rapid
Repair services	5.2	6.9	32.7	Moderate
Personal services	28.9	14.7	-49.1	Declining
Other services	10.3	10.3	0.0	Stagnant
Total	100.0%	100.0%		

* Excludes agriculture, medicine, and law.
** Definitions of terms used to describe industry growth rates and industries with those growth rates: *Rapid*—over 50 percent increase in the incidence of self-employment (transportation, communication, FIRE, business service, wholesale); *Moderate*—10 to 50 percent increase in the incidence of self-employment (manufacturing, repair services); *Stagnant*—minus 10 to plus 10 percent change in the incidence of self-employment (retail, construction, other services); *Declining*—over 10 percent decrease in the incidence of self-employment (personal services).

rapidly. *Editorial note: In this study, "minority" referred to blacks, Hispanics, Asians, and Native Americans.*

27. Frank Fratoe and Ronald Meeks. *Business Participation Rates and Self-Employment Incomes: An Analysis of the 50 Largest Ancestry Groups.* Los Angeles: UCLA Center for Afro-American Studies, 1988.

• Fratoe and Meeks studied self-employed persons who reported a single ancestry group. All of them had filled out the 1980 Census of Population long form. For the 50 largest ancestry groups, the authors cross-tabulated ancestry group by self-employment to ascertain the business participation rate for each group, that rate being defined as the number of self-employed persons per 1,000 population of a group. Similarly, they also cross-tabulated ancestry by income of persons reporting self-employed status ("income" here refers to a person's total money income from all sources).

Fratoe and Meeks found that 4.9 percent of all persons reporting a single ancestry group were self-employed in 1980; their mean income was $18,630 (total), of which $13,960 was mean (nonfarm) self-employment income. Business participation rates ranged from a high of 117.4 persons per 1,000 for Russians to a low of 10.6 per 1,000 for Puerto Ricans. Other than Puerto Ricans, the groups reporting the lowest business participation rates (more than 50 percent below the U.S. average) were Sub-Saharan African, Dominican, Haitian, Vietnamese, Mexican, Hawaiian, Jamaican, Filipino, and Ecuadorian. Among the predominantly black ancestry groups, business participation rates were:

Sub-Saharan African	13.6	persons per 1,000
Dominican	14.6	"
Haitian	15.5	"
Jamaican	21.5	"

In other words, among every 1,000 sub-Saharan Africans, fewer than 14 reported being self-employed. Among all ancestry groups, 48.9 of every 1,000 persons reported being self-employed.

Among the self-employed, group mean incomes varied widely, ranging from $11,260 for sub-Saharan Africans to $31,370 for Iranians. For nonfarm self-employment income only, mean income ranged from

$9,150 for Vietnamese to $22,240 for Asian Indians. Among predominantly black groups, mean nonfarm self-employment incomes were:

Sub-Saharan African	$ 9,830
Dominican	$10,480
Jamaican	$12,490
Haitian	$12,820

The groups whose self-employed members have low mean incomes are generally the groups with low business participation rates. Of the 10 groups with the lowest mean incomes, eight were also among the bottom 10 in business participation rates (Sub-Saharan African, Puerto Rican, Vietnamese, Ecuadorian, Mexican, Dominican, Hawaiian, and Jamaican). Of the 10 groups with the highest mean incomes, five were among the top 10 in business participation rates (Russian, Rumanian, Austrian, Lebanese, and Syrian). Using a rank-order correlation measure (Spearman's rho), Fratoe and Meeks calculated a correlation of .61 (statistically significant at the 1 percent level) between business participation rate and mean income.

With only a few exceptions, the ancestry groups least active in self-employment were also the least successful (as measured by mean incomes).

28. Robert Suggs. "Recent Changes in Black-Owned Business." Joint Center for Political Studies Working Paper. Washington, D.C.: 1986.

• This paper, which analyzed Census Bureau survey data of all black-owned small businesses that filed tax returns, indicated that the number of black firms grew substantially between 1977 and 1982. The high rate of growth in firm numbers, however, was not indicative of business progress. More pertinent measures of business performance indicated that black business receipts deteriorated seriously and that the number of persons employed was stagnant.

Using data from the 1977 and 1982 Census Bureau Survey of Minority-Owned Business Enterprise, Suggs identified 89 industries in which black business sales exceeded $15 million nationwide in 1982. Between 1977 and 1982, average receipts per firm increased in 29 of the industries and declined in the other 60. In his comparison of the growing and declining industry groups, Suggs observed a "peculiar pattern of growth and decline that merits examination: Why did black firms experience solid growth in industries where blacks in the past had been few and far between, while firms in industries where black businesses had long been significant were declining?" (p. 24). Within selected services, for example, black-owned firms have traditionally been concentrated in personal services, an area that declined precipitously. In contrast, business services grew quite rapidly: "Its receipts grew 124 percent in 10 years and its employment nearly doubled" (p. 8). Large black-owned firms (more than 100 employees) generally grew rapidly; they accounted for 90 percent of the increase in employment in black-owned firms. The largest black-owned firms grew faster than the rest of the economy, doubling their sales (in constant dollars) between 1972 and 1982.

Suggs concluded that the entire black business community lost ground between 1977 and 1982 in relation to business as a whole and in absolute revenue dollars. In addition, this overall decline masked an important diverging trend. On the one hand, a large part of the black business community, which developed under pervasive racial segregation, is declining. On the other hand, "a newer and smaller group of black entrepreneurs appears to be benefiting from new opportunities derived from Civil Rights advances. Their firms are making gains in industries where blacks have traditionally been excluded" (p. 31).

Why the decline in traditional strongholds of black business? Desegregation in housing, the work place, and public accommodations widened the retail market for black consumers and disbursed them geographically. Desegregation does not, however, require whites to patronize black firms. Many of the traditional black firms, long excluded from the mainstream economy, were ill-equipped to exploit the new opportunities desegregation offered. "Therefore, instead of expanding from its existing base, black business capable of competing in a unitary economy may be developing from scratch" (p. vii).

29. Timothy Bates. "Traditional and Emerging Lines of Black Business Enterprise." Chapter 2 in *Banking on Black Enterprise*. Washington, D.C.: Joint Center for Political and Economic Studies, 1992 (forthcoming)

• Black firms in the 1980s continued to be heavily overrepresented in small-scale traditional lines of business. The Characteristics of Business Owners data base, which is compiled by the U.S. Bureau of the Census, shows that 56.2 percent of all black-owned firms reported annual sales of less than $25,000 in 1982. Further, 75.4 percent of the same firms had no paid employees. White firms, in contrast, were more than three times as likely to be in the $200,000 plus annual sales groupings; only 4.8 percent of black firms achieved sales of $200,000 or more in 1982.

The most comprehensive and up-to-date sources—such as the 1982 CBO survey—do indeed highlight the marginal nature of the majority of black-owned firms. It is, however, invalid to generalize about the nature of black enterprise solely by observing cross-sectional data that highlight the weaker businesses. Most personal service and small-scale retail enterprises owned by nonminorities are marginal operations, too. The numerous struggling enterprises that typify much of the nation's small business sector frequently offer paltry returns to the self-employed; consequently, failure rates are quite high irrespective of the owner's racial background.

Although marginal business operations are undoubtedly numerous within the black business community, the data reveal a clear trend toward more skill-intensive lines of business. In 1960, nearly 30 percent of self-employed blacks ran personal services firms and fewer than 10 percent operated in skill-intensive areas such as FIRE, business services, and professional services. According to the CBO, among the business start-ups in the 1976-1982 time period, 25 percent were in skill-intensive service industries, and only 10.3 percent were in personal services. Thirty years ago, blacks in skill-intensive areas were concentrated in a few specialties: medicine, law, and insurance. Today, the list of specialties has broadened to include consulting firms, advertising agencies, engineering services, accounting agencies, employment agencies, computer software firms, and so forth. The CBO data on black business reflect trends toward diversity that are vitally important for comprehending the trajectory of black entrepreneurship.

30. Peter Bearse. "An Econometric Analysis of Black Entrepreneurship." *The Review of Black Political Economy* **12 (Spring 1984).**

• Part of the uniqueness of the black entrepreneur pool lies in the fact that the proportion of the black labor force pursuing self-employment is quite low relative to the proportion of whites. Bearse, using a 1976 national data source, found that among labor force members over 21 years of age, 12.3 percent of whites and 3.6 percent of blacks were self-employed. Among all minorities (including those 21 years of age and under), the percentages of self-employed persons were: blacks, 3.26 percent; Hispanics, 5.52 percent; and Asians, 8.38 percent.

Bearse identified several traits that accounted for the higher incidences of white and Asian self-employment. First, he found that high levels of educational attainment improved the likelihood of self-employment; this factor was strongly positive for whites and Asians, slightly weaker for blacks. Second, a complex variable measuring asset holdings also explained the higher proportion of white and Asian entrepreneurs relative to black entrepreneurs. Larger asset holdings appear to be causally related to higher incidences of entrepreneurship, and blacks lagged behind all other groups regarding size of assets. Finally, he found that part of the particularly low incidence rate for black self-employment was rooted in opportunity cost considerations: high alternative earning opportunities appeared to particularly discourage better educated blacks from pursuing self-employment. (For a definition of opportunity cost, see Appendix C.)

31. Richard Stevens. "Measuring Minority Business Formation and Failure." *The Review of Black Political Economy* **12 (Spring 1984).**

• This study investigated possible causes of minorities' relatively low rates of business ownership. Among nonminorities, the small business participation rate is about 63 persons per 1,000; among minorities, the rate is only 14 per 1,000. Disaggregation revealed that participation rates for the minority groups are highest for Asians and lowest for blacks (Hispanics were in the middle).

Stevens hypothesized that minorities have both a lower business formation rate and a higher failure rate than nonminorities. Although appropriate data for nonminorities were unavailable, the Census Bureau constructed a special data file containing 336,997 minority firms existing in 1972, and Stevens compared this to a similarly comprehensive file of 402,924 minority firms existing in 1977. This exercise produced estimated rates of firm formation and discontinuance over the 1972-77 time period; the rates are summarized below:

	Annual formation rate	Annual discontinuance rate
Black	14.9%	12.3%
Hispanic	17.2	13.9
Asian	20.7	12.3

These numbers suggest that in the average year between 1972 and 1977, the number of black firms formed was equal to 14.9 percent of the total number of black firms that existed in 1972. Similarly, the number of discontinuances was equal to 12.3 percent of the number of black firms that existed in 1972. Relative to the 1972 base, the number of black firms increased by a net of 2.6 percent (14.9 minus12.3) per year through 1977. The corresponding net annual rate of increase among Asians, in contrast, was 8.4 percent (20.7 minus 12.3). The noteworthy fact is that Asians and blacks had identical discontinuance rates. The high growth rate among Asian firms, therefore, was attributed *entirely* to their higher formation rate relative to blacks.

Stevens' findings are provocative, but the author cautioned that discontinuance was overestimated somewhat in this study. For example, two or more of the firms in the 1972 file could have merged during the five year interval, but they most likely would have been counted as discontinuances in 1977 due to the inability to track mergers (as well as buyouts) in the file. Another example is that a growing firm that was formerly tracked by owner social security number might obtain an employer ID number. (Firms that do not have employer ID numbers are tracked by owner social security number.) A change from social security number in 1972 to employer ID number in 1977 would cause the firm to be counted as a discontinuance in 1977.

These biases notwithstanding, Stevens did highlight the much greater range of formation rates—as opposed to the more consistent discontinuance rates—that is typical of minority firms across racial and ethnic groups. The same pattern is typical within industry groups. Formation and discontinuance rates for three industries are summarized below to illustrate this pattern.

	Formation rate	Discontinuance rate
1. Growth: business services	23.1%	13.1%
2. Stable: food stores	13.7	12.9
3. Declining: auto dealers	10.5	14.0

These rates were calculated from the same minority business file cited above. Differences between growing and declining industries are captured most directly by formation rate differentials; discontinuance rate differentials are relatively minor. The obvious policy implication is that minority business development depends vitally on the rate at which new firms are formed.

32. Frank Fratoe. "Social Capital and Small Business Owners." *The Review of Black Political Economy* **16 (Spring 1988).**

• In the sociological approach to analyzing minority business, firm ownership was treated as a group phenomenon, heavily dependent on the social resources available from group support networks. The entrepreneur is seen as a member of supportive networks—kinship, peer, and community groups—which, in turn, help create and operate small businesses by providing social resources, or social capital, such as financial support, sources of labor, customers, role models, and so forth.

Fratoe hypothesized that the lower incidence of self-employment among blacks may be rooted in the lower levels of social capital available from their support networks. He derived measures of social capital from the CBO data base and compared the incidence of those measures across groups of self-employed black, Asian, Hispanic, and nonminority males.

Fratoe first examined role models: "the relative absence of early positive role models can result in a dampening effect on the formation of entrepreneurs within a group" (p. 36). He found that a smaller percentage of black business owners have parents or close relatives who are self-employed (21 percent) than Asians (32.8 percent) and nonminorities (38.5 percent).

Another key function of support groups is to provide capital to finance business formations. Fratoe found that Asians are much more likely than others to rely on family and friends for business start-up capital. Hispanics ranked second in terms of using this type of social capital, and nonminorities ranked third. Blacks are least likely to receive start-up capital from family and friends. Nonminorities use commercial bank loans at a disproportionately higher rate than minorities. Blacks use no financial capital sources disproportionately.

He found that black firms rely on minority customers and employees much more heavily than any of the other groups. Asian firms were found to rely less on minority employees and much less on minority customers than black and Hispanic firms.

Editorial note: Whereas Fratoe compiled certain measures of social capital, he did not investigate whether the measures were, in fact, causally related to survival, size, profitability or other firm traits associated with viability. These issues are discussed more extensively later in this volume, under the section entitled, "Asian and Hispanic Self-Employment," which begins on page 56.

Small Business in General

This brief section focuses on recent analyses of nonminority firms that are highly relevant to minority business issues. Boyan Jovanovic (no. 33), David Evans (no. 34a), and Timothy Bates and Alfred Nucci (34b) have argued that business failure is heavily concentrated among the youngest and smallest firms. Minority-owned firms are disproportionately smaller and younger than nonminority firms, thus minority firms very frequently exhibit the traits associated with high failure rates. Evans and Linda Leighton (no. 35) examined the issue of who chooses self-employment (as opposed to employee status); low entry rates are thought to be highly important in explaining the relatively low incidence of blacks and Hispanics in small business.

Bates (nos. 36 and 37) further examined the issue of small business discontinuance. Very low levels of financial capital investment at the point of business start-up are associated with small firm size: minimal capital leads to tiny firms. The small firms least likely to survive are those newly formed by persons with low levels of education who invest small amounts of financial capital in their ventures. Conversely, the firms most likely to survive are those formed by college educated persons who start out investing substantial financial capital.

Finally, Lawrence White (no. 38) identified the types of manufacturing industries that are most likely to attract small firms. They found that they tend to be labor intensive, high-growth industries that serve local markets.

33. Boyan Jovanovic. "Selection and Evolution in Industry." *Econometrica* 50 (May 1982).

• Jovanovic developed a model of small business behavior that assumes that entrepreneurs are typically uncertain about their managerial abilities when they enter self-employment. The behavior of young firms varies more (and includes higher failure rates) than that of older firms, because the owners' estimates of their abilities are not precise. Owners gradually learn about their managerial abilities by running the business and observing how well they do. As their learning progresses, they acquire increasingly precise estimates of their abilities, and the firm's costs of doing business vary less. And as owners learn more about their abilities, their behavior changes: those who revise their estimates of their ability upward tend to expand output, whereas those who revise their ability estimates downward tend to contract or to dissolve their businesses: "efficient firms grow and survive: the inefficient decline and fail" (p. 650).

34a. David Evans. "The Relationship Between Firm Growth, Size and Age: Estimates for 100 Manufacturing Industries." *The Journal of Industrial Economics* **35 (June 1987).**

34b. Timothy Bates and Alfred Nucci. "An Analysis of Small Business Size and Rate of Discontinuance." *Journal of Small Business Management* **27 (October 1989).**

• Evans found that the survival rates of firms of all sizes in 100 manufacturing industries are a function of size (in terms of sales revenues) and age: the older firms with larger sales revenues are most likely to remain in business.

Bates and Nucci examined data that typify all small firms, and their findings were identical to those of Evans. Bates and Nucci used the 1982 Characteristics of Business Owners data base, which included 86,118 small firms. It was a representative sample of firms in all lines of business. For all 86,118 firms, Bates and Nucci calculated business survival rates based on whether the individual firms in the sample were still operating in late 1986; the results are summarized below:

1982 total sales revenue	Percentage of firms in this size category discontinuing operations by late 1986
All firms with sales under $50,000	39.1
All firms with sales of $50,000 and up	15.1

Bates and Nucci then compared the firms started before 1976 (older firms) and those started between 1976 and 1982 (younger firms). They found that the younger firms:

- were more likely to have discontinued operations by late 1986,
- had smaller 1982 mean annual sales, and
- were more dispersed around the mean values of sales.

Finally, the authors controlled econometrically for firm age, and they found a very strong, direct relationship between sales revenue and the likelihood of continuing business operations. Age notwithstanding, the firms with larger sales revenues were most likely to remain in business.

35. David Evans and Linda Leighton. "Some Empirical Aspects of Entrepreneurship." American Economic Review 79 (June 1989).

• The fraction of the labor force that is self-employed has increased since the mid-1970s. This study attempted to identify the traits of white males who are likely to choose self-employment as opposed to employee status. Utilizing the National Longitudinal Survey of Young Men as well as Current Population Surveys, Evans and Leighton found that:

- the fraction of the labor force that is self-employed increases with age until the early 40s and then it remains constant until the retirement years, when it begins to drop;
- the probability of departing from self-employment decreases with duration in self-employment: about half of entrants return to employee status within seven years;
- men with greater assets are more likely than those with fewer assets to switch to self-employment;
- controlling for asset level, unemployed workers, men who have changed jobs a lot, and lower paid workers are more likely to enter self-employment;
- other things being equal, college graduates are more likely to pursue self-employment.

36. Timothy Bates. "Entrepreneur Factor Inputs and Small Business Longevity" (discussion paper). Washington, D.C.: U.S. Bureau of the Census, Center for Economic Studies, June 1989.

• Very small firms consistently have high rates of discontinuance, and black-owned firms are much smaller, on average, than white-owned firms. Microeconomic theories of firm behavior view businesses as producing outputs, quantities of which are a function of labor and capital input levels:

output = F(labor inputs, capital inputs)

Because marginal products associated with these factor inputs are assumed to be positive, incremental labor and capital inputs increase output. In other words, high quantities of labor and capital provide the resources that generate high sales levels; low levels of labor and capital production produce low sales levels.

Blacks firms typically have lower sales levels than white firms because the owners invest smaller amounts of financial capital, spend fewer hours working per week, have less managerial experience, and generally have lower levels of educational attainment. When all of these factors are considered simultaneously, the smaller amounts of financial capital investment emerge as the principal explanation for the lower sales levels of black firms. Low levels of financial capital investment have produced an abundance of very small black enterprises. It has also led to discontinuance rates that are high relative to those among white-owned businesses.

37. Timothy Bates. "Entrepreneur Human Capital Inputs and Small Business Longevity." *The Review of Economics and Statistics 72* **(November 1990).**

• This study used CBO data describing firms formed by white males during the 1976-1982 period. Econometric techniques were used to identify the characteristics of businesses and the traits of owners that are associated with firm survival. As expected, it was found that the firms least likely to remain in business are those that have operated for three years or less (young firms). The firms most likely to survive had highly educated entrepreneurs (four or more years of college) and larger financial capital inputs at start-up.

For the 32 percent of businesses that were launched with bank financing, having a highly educated owner was clearly associated with investing substantial sums of capital in one's business. College graduates, in other words, have greater access to debt capital, which helps them establish larger firms. Leverage notwithstanding, the two owner traits most strongly linked to firm viability are (1) college graduate and (2) substantial financial investment. Irrespective of financial capital source, the owner education and financial capital input variables consistently explained firm longevity.

38. Lawrence White. "The Determinants of the Relative Importance of Small Business." *The Review of Economics and Statistics* 54 (February 1982).

• Why does small business flourish in some industry sectors but not in others? White studied this issue by investigating the question: Why is the minimum efficient business size relatively small in some industries and relatively large in others? Due to data restrictions, White analyzed manufacturing firms only. He examined determinants of minimum efficient firm size for 115 different manufacturing industry groups. Specifically, where economies of large scale production are present, small firms were expected to be rare. White defined small manufacturing firms as those having under $5 million in sales in 1972: these small firms accounted for 13.8 percent of all manufacturing sales in the United States.

White's empirical analysis of 1972 data revealed that small manufacturing firms are most prevalent in industries with low capital to labor ratios, low vertical integration, fast growth, localized markets, and greater sales of producer goods than consumer goods. (For a definition of vertical integration see Appendix C.) Except for the vertical integration factor, the results were statistically significant. White found that labor intensive manufacturing firms in high growth industries tend to be disproportionately small. Furthermore, smaller firms are relatively more frequent in industries where most sales are made locally (rather than in the national or interstate markets) and where sales are made largely to other firms (not to consumers). Surprisingly, small manufacturing firms did not seem to be adversely affected in industries in which intensive advertising is important. The major single barrier to small firms was found to be capital intensity: Relatively high capital requirements are associated with greatly reduced small business presence.

The Role of Human Capital

Highly educated minorities tend to create more substantive, profitable firms, and they were responsible for much of the growth in the minority business sector over the past two decades, according to studies by Swinton and Handy and by Bates. Minority college enrollments have increased substantially since the 1960s, and this growth has co-existed with a substantial shift towards minorities majoring in business-related fields. Despite some very minor declines in the attendance rates of black and Hispanic males in the 1980s, minority student enrollments continue to grow in absolute terms, particularly among Hispanics. Possessing a college degree has been most rewarding for self-employed minorities concentrating in skill-intensive service fields such as professional services, business services, and finance, insurance, and real estate.

College graduates rarely enter less remunerative fields such as personal services and small-scale retailing. Asians are an exception. Asians, however, tend to leave fields such as retailing; they are much more likely to remain self-employed in skill-intensive industries such as professional services.

39. David Swinton and John Handy. *The Determinants of the Growth of Black-Owned Businesses: A Preliminary Analysis.* Washington, D.C.: U.S. Department of Commerce, Minority Business Development Agency, 1983.

• The findings of this study emphasized the importance of highly educated and trained persons in explaining the growth of black entrepreneurship. According to Handy and Swinton, three closely interrelated variables most accurately predicted growth in the number of black-owned firms between 1972 and 1977 at the Standard Metropolitan Statistical Area (SMSA) level: (1) growth in the available pool of professional and managerial labor force participants; (2) the number of persons in professional and managerial occupations in 1972; (3) the level of black education within the SMSA.

40. Timothy Bates. "Entrepreneur Human Capital and Minority Business Viability." The Journal of Human Resources 20 (Fall 1985).

• Clearly, one of the major reasons for the high retention rates (and low failure rates) of better educated black entrepreneurs lies in their high self-employment incomes. This study of Dun's Financial Profile data found that the fields that attract minorities with above average educations are highly profitable relative to the other fields that attract minorities. Of the minority firms in the Dun and Bradstreet sample, 35.8 percent belonged to the high-education lines of business, and their median after-tax profits were $39,974, versus $29,308 for the other firms. Controlling for corporate status, net worth level, and macroeconomic conditions in the context of a regression model explaining profits, Bates found that the net profits of the median high-education firm (total assets of $339,473) were $12,560 higher than they were for the other firms.

41. Timothy Bates. "Characteristics of Minorities Who Are Entering Self-Employment." *The Review of Black Political Economy* **15 (Fall 1986).**

• This study found that employees who pursue self-employment on a part-time basis ("employee" is their main labor force status) have been a particularly important factor in upgrading the status of the minority entrepreneur universe over the long-term. A sample of 4,031 minority "part-timers" was drawn from the public use sample of the 1980 Census, and they were found to be younger, have much better educations, and have higher incomes relative to the overall minority entrepreneur universe. In comparing them to all self-employed minorities under age 65, this study found that:

- 58 percent of the part-timers had attended college, compared to 34 percent of other minority entrepreneurs;
- 37 percent of the part-timers had graduated from college, compared to 15 percent of other minority entrepreneurs;
- 3.6 percent of the part-timers ran personal service firms, compared to 14.3 percent of other minority entrepreneurs;
- the average age of the part-timers was 38.6 years, compared to 41.7 for the other minority entrepreneurs;
- the average income from all sources was $18,707 for the part-timers, compared to $13,570 for other minority entrepreneurs.

42a. John Reid. "Black America in the 1980s." *Population Bulletin* 37 (December 1983).

42b. William Trent. "Equity Considerations in Higher Education: Race and Sex Differences in Degree Attainment and Major Field from 1976 through 1981." *American Journal of Education* 41 (May 1984).

• The incidence of black entrepreneurship should continue to increase in the future if highly educated younger blacks are attracted to self-employment. College enrollments by black students increased dramatically in the 1960s and 1970s, and enrollment growth in business-related fields has been particularly rapid. The incidence of black college enrollment, for example, rose from 10.3 percent in 1965 to 19.4 percent in 1981 for those age 18 to 24 years (Reid). Educational achievements have translated into occupational and earnings gains, especially among young minority college graduates. In 1959, black male college graduates age 25 to 34 years earned only 59 percent of what their white college cohorts earned; by 1979, the figure had jumped to 84 percent. Interest in business studies increased between 1976 and 1981, as black college students tended to major less often in the fields of education and social science (Trent).

43. American Council on Education. *Seventh Annual Status Report.* Washngton, D.C.: 1988.

• This report summarized information on high school completion and college participation rates for 18-to-24-year-olds. The largest part of the report consists of tables of data summarizing enrollment patterns and levels of educational attainment for groups defined by sex, race, and ethnicity. The structure lends itself to a "calculate your own statistics, draw your own conclusions" approach. An essential starting point for anyone wishing to comprehend the diverse data is the table of statistics on high school graduation rates for 18-to-24-year-olds. The data on high school graduation rates are summarized below:

| | High school graduation rate | |
	1976	1986
White	82.4%	83.1%
Black	67.5	76.4
Hispanic	55.6	59.9

The proportion of high school graduates from 1976 to 1986 was obviously fairly stable for whites; however, it increased quite substantially for blacks and less so for Hispanics.

Based on the method chosen, it is possible to document three distinct trends in black college enrollment rates between 1976 and 1986.

Trend One: College enrollment is up among blacks. Here the "attended college" rate is found by calculating the percentage of blacks 18-to-24 years of age who are presently enrolled in college and those who have completed one or more years of college. In 1976 and 1986, the percentages were as follows:

1976	34.0%
1986	36.2%

In 1986, 36.2 percent of blacks in this age bracket had attended or were attending college, up from a corresponding figure of 34.0 percent in 1976.

Trend Two: College enrollment is down among blacks. Using this method, the attended college rate is derived by calculating the percentages of high school graduates who attend college. In 1976 and 1986, the percentages were as follows:

	Whites	Blacks
1976	53.5%	50.4%
1986	55.3	47.4

From 1976 to 1986, the percentage fell among blacks, whereas it increased among whites.

Trend three: College enrollment is relatively stable among blacks. This conclusion can be reached by using the "college participation" rate rather than the "attended college" rate that was used to document the first two trends. The college participation rate measures 18-to-24-year-olds who are actually enrolled in college during October of a specific year (such as 1986). For all blacks 18-to-24 years of age, the relevant college participation rates were as follows:

1976	22.6%
1986	21.9

The main reason for these diverging trends lies in the large increase in black high school graduation rates over the 1976-1986 period. Thus, the percentage of blacks attending college increased, as documented by method one; however, because of the higher high school graduation rate, the percentage of black high school graduates attending college fell. Other possibly relevant factors include a slight shift from four-year institutions to two-year colleges (which lowers the overall college participation rate but not the attended college rate) and a decline in college enrollment among black males. Disaggregating method three by sex, for example, yields the following black college participation rates:

	Males	Females
1976	22.0%	23.0%
1986	20.0	23.4

College participation rates among Hispanics are similarly subject to definitional fluidity, and they also exhibit trends that differ across the sexes: participation appears to be up for females in both relative and absolute terms; for Hispanic males, participation is up in absolute terms and down in relative terms.

44. Timothy Bates. *An Analysis of Income Differentials Among Self-Employed Minorities.* Los Angeles: UCLA Center for Afro-American Studies, 1988.

• Minority entrepreneurs who are highly educated tend to earn higher financial returns when they gravitate toward certain skill-intensive lines of business. Possessing a college degree is particularly rewarding for minorities pursuing self-employment in finance, insurance, and real estate; professional services; business services; and transportation and communication. In the professional services, the financial return to college educated entrepreneurs is especially substantial. A high school diploma appears to be adequate preparation for self-employment in construction and personal services. In industries such as construction, the best route beyond high school may be to gain work experience or training through programs such as apprenticeships.

Among Asians and Hispanics in particular, self-employed males with only elementary educations suffer severe income losses relative to high school graduates. The least educated group contains a high proportion of immigrant entrepreneurs, and their earnings losses may be rooted in language difficulties. Self-employed Asians and Hispanics also pay less attention than blacks to the opportunity costs of self-employment. One manifestation of this is their tendency to cling to self-employment even if their own labor incomes are low and wage employment would offer higher potential earnings. This relative indifference to the opportunity costs of self-employment may reflect, once again, a high incidence of language difficulties, which limits their wage employment opportunities.

45. Timothy Bates. "Why Black Firms Fail." Chapter 3 in *Banking on Black Enterprise*. Washington, D.C.: Joint Center for Political and Economic Studies, 1992 (forthcoming).

• The educational backgrounds of black entrepreneurs are closely related to the lines of business that they enter. College graduates seldom enter into traditional fields such as personal services—an industry in which black-owned firms rarely use paid employees. Instead, highly educated entrepreneurs invest in larger scale industries such as wholesaling, where growth prospects are greater, owner remuneration is above average, and the use of paid employees is the norm. In those rare instances where college graduates do enter into smaller scale traditional lines of business, the firms they establish are no more likely to last than the ones established by high school dropouts.

The case of Asian-owned retail operations is enlightening in this context. Highly educated Asian immigrants entered retailing in very large numbers during the 1980s. Furthermore, they crowded into the smaller scale, less profitable lines of retailing such as food stores and restaurants. Asians are underrepresented, relative to nonminorities, in the larger scale fields such as building materials, new car dealerships, and appliance stores. Therefore, the mean 1982 sales for Asian-owned retailing firms formed between 1976 and 1982—$137,369—lagged predictably behind the mean 1982 sales for nonminority retail enterprises—$175,509 (these figures were computed from the CBO data base, described in Appendix B). Firm profitability is lower in retailing than in any other line of Asian-owned business. The combination of language barriers and financial capital constraints causes highly educated Asian immigrants to enter low-yielding retail enterprises. Many of the operations fail outright shortly after they are created. Yet, even the "successful" operations tend to lose their founders. As they improve their English fluency and accumulate financial resources, the barriers that dictated self-employment in retailing ease. Therefore, the owners leave retailing, opting instead for opportunities that permit them to use their human capital more fully and, hence, to generate higher remuneration. The lines of self-employment that retain highly educated Asians are those that offer both the opportunity to use one's professional skills and training and the expectation of high levels of remuneration.

The Role of Financial Capital

The difficulties for self-employed minorities in breaking into large-scale emerging lines of business are a reflection of constraints deeply rooted in U.S. society. The minority business community has been shaped by limited access to credit, limited educational and training opportunities, and other constraints. Several key limitations have changed in the last 25 years, thus easing traditional barriers to progress. Government loans became available to actual and prospective minority entrepreneurs in the late 1960s. The availability of government loan guarantees (against default risk) induced many banks to extend business loans, thus eroding a tradition of minimal contact between minorities (blacks most especially), and commercial bank lending departments. Minority college enrollments increased dramatically in the 1960s and 1970s, especially in business-related fields. These trends are highly interrelated, because minority entrepreneurs with college educations have the greatest access to traditional financial capital sources such as commercial banks.

Major barriers to progress in emerging lines of business remain, nonetheless, and they continue to complicate minority enterprise development, particularly among blacks. The major constraint upon black business formation, growth, and diversification in the 1980s was rooted in capitalization problems. Lack of personal wealth holdings combined with discriminatory treatment by commercial banks spelled continuing obstacles to firm formation, survival, and growth for many potential and actual black entrepreneurs. Hispanic and Asian business owners appear to have been less severely impacted by capital constraints.

The first four studies in this section document that the household wealth holdings of blacks and Hispanics (but not Asians) lag quite substantially behind those of nonminority households. Lacking equity, many of the largest minority-owned firms have necessarily relied very heavily on debt to finance growth. The study by Development Through Applied Science (no. 50) shows that this debt reliance frequently caused very high leverage among the large-scale minority firms.

Whereas high leverage was typical among the largest minority firms, the broader population of small- and medium-sized minority firms faced restricted access to debt. A study by Bates (no. 51) shows that black business start-ups utilize vastly less debt than nonminority business start-ups. Faith Ando (no. 52) found that black-owned firms have much less access to bank loans than nonminority firms. Even when business risk is controlled for, blacks have much less success than nonminorities in obtaining bank loans. Robert Edelstein (no. 53a) claimed that underfunding black businesses causes high default rates. Timothy Bates and Donald Hester (no. 53b) while not disagreeing with Edelstein, charged that he failed to prove his point.

Commercial banks are the largest single loan source for small business. In an analysis of 28 large metropolitan areas, Bates (no. 54) showed that banks' willingness to lend is heavily influenced by geographic location: if the borrower's firm is located in a minority community, loan size is cut drastically. Finally, Gavin Chen and John Cole (no. 55) argued that not all minority groups are similarly disadvantaged: blacks have less access to financial capital than Asian and Hispanics.

Wealth Holdings

46. Henry Terrell. "Wealth Accumulation of Black and White Families." *Journal of Finance* 26 (May 1971).

• Personal wealth holdings are traditionally the major source of capital for creating and expanding small businesses. Herein lies an essential element for comprehending development patterns among black businesses. Terrell's study of nationwide wealth holdings showed that, on average, black families have less than one-fifth the holdings of white families. The forms in which wealth is held also differ dramatically. For example:

- 64.4 percent of aggregate black wealth holdings represent equity in homes, cars, and trucks; the corresponding figure for whites is 37.4 percent.
- 10.2 percent of aggregate black wealth holdings are in the form of financial assets, compared to 30.1 percent for whites.
- 5.7 percent of aggregate black wealth holdings represent equity in small businesses, compared to 9.4 percent for whites.

If we exclude blacks in low-income brackets and focus only on those earning over $20,000 annually, we find that the average for wealth holdings is $30,195 per household—roughly 30 percent of the average of $101,009 reported by all whites earning over $20,000 per year. Blacks collectively (those earning more and less than $20,000 annually) have very small wealth holdings relative to whites. Furthermore, most of their wealth is held in nonbusiness and nonfinancial forms. White households not only hold, on average, more than five times as much wealth as blacks, but they also hold more of their aggregate wealth in the form of business equity and financial assets (39.5 percent vs. 15.9 percent for blacks).

47. Peter Bearse. *An Econometric Analysis of Minority Entrepreneurship.* Washington, D.C.: U.S. Department of Commerce, Minority Business Development Agency, 1983.

• Data for 1977 on 16 types of wealth (but not total wealth) indicate that the household wealth holdings of Asians are, on average, roughly equal to the household wealth holdings of nonminorities. Hispanics, in contrast, lag far behind nonminorities in mean wealth per household, but they are slightly ahead of blacks. It is clear that blacks collectively have very little aggregate wealth relative to whites to invest in business creation and expansion.

48a. "Survey of Consumer Finances, 1983." *Federal Reserve Bulletin* **70 (September 1984).**

48b. "Survey of Consumer Finances, 1983: A Second Report." *Federal Reserve Bulletin* **70 (December 1984).**

holdings of nonminorities.

• In 1984, the Federal Reserve System created a new data source on family wealth holdings. Published reports describing these data contain some detail on black wealth holdings. According to these two recently published reports summarizing parts of the data, minority wealth holdings predictably lag dramatically behind the

	Household net worth, 1983	
	(Median)	(Mean)
Caucasian	$31,904	$74,743
Nonwhite and Hispanic	$ 1,353	$27,605

	Percentage of households owning business assets, 1983
Caucasian	16%
Nonwhite and Hispanic	7%

The usefulness of these data is compromised because they contain no breakdowns into black, Hispanic, and Asian subgroupings. At the level of generality represented above, the data are totally consistent with the 1971 data represented in the Terrell study above and the more recent data presented below.

49. William D. Bradford. "Wealth, Assets, and Income in Black Households." *Afro-American Studies Program Working Paper, Vol. 1, No. 1.* **University of Maryland, February 1990.**

• More recent data on family wealth holdings in 1984 indicate that black households had a median net worth of $3,397, compared to $39,135 for white households: in other words, for every one dollar of wealth in the median white family, the median black family had nine cents (Jaynes and Williams 1989). According to this study, whereas only 8.6 percent of the white households had zero or negative net worth, 31 percent of the black households held absolutely no wealth. Wealth in the form of small business equity was most commonly observed among black households with incomes exceeding $24,000: 3.5 percent of black upper middle income ($24,000 - $48,000) households and 14.0 percent of the black high-income households held business equity. The percentage of white households with business equity ownership surpassed that of black households at every income level. At the upper-middle and high income levels, respectively, 11.0 percent and 21.6 percent of white households held wealth in the form of small business equity. The greatest disparity in business equity holdings, however, derived from the fact that higher income white households are relatively much more numerous than higher income black households.

Disparities in personal wealth holdings therefore continue to handicap black business start-ups today. In the 1980s, black business creation was heavily concentrated in industries where formation required relatively little financial capital. Lacking assets and therefore borrowing capacities, blacks are ill-equipped to cope with economic adversities and to exploit economic opportunities.

Editorial Note: This paper is cited extensively in A Common Destiny, *edited by Gerald Jaynes and Robin Williams, which is reviewed later in this bibliography (no. 67).*

Debt and Leverage

50. Development Through Applied Science (DETAS). *New Perspectives on Minority Business Development.* **Washington, D.C.: U.S. Department of Commerce, Minority Business Develoment Agency, 1983.**

• This study used data from Dun and Bradstreet's Dun's Financial Profile (DFP) to investigate balance sheet and income statement figures for a sample of large scale minority-owned businesses. Because the firms in the sample tended to be larger and more established than those in the universe, they represent a more successful subset of the minority business community.

The DETAS study calculated linear regression models to explain after-tax profits for the sample of minority firms. Parallel analyses were conducted for a comparison group of nonminority firms drawn from DFP data. Finally, statistical analyses of business discontinuance were conducted for the minority and nonminority firms. The findings may be summarized as follows:

- Large-scale minority firms usually maintain highly leveraged positions, reflected in their lower net worth to total asset ratios. Further investigation of the balance sheet revealed that the greater leverage of minority firms was caused by their heavy reliance on long-term debt relative to the nonminority sample. But borrowing long-term, while profitable for many minority businesses, is not without its risks, since highly leveraged firms are more vulnerable to sustained periods of low profit, such as occurs during recessions. The heavier reliance on debt rather than on net worth is likely to generate more failures among minority firms during recessions relative to their less-leveraged nonminority counterparts. This conclusion was reinforced by the results of the discriminant analyses, which indicated that the incidence of zero or negative profits for minority firms is four times that of their nonminority counterparts.
- The analysis of discontinuances suggested that the firms that discontinued operations were relatively illiquid, had low net worths, and were disproportionately concentrated in the retail trade sector.
- A study of life cycle characteristics of minority-owned firms indicated that size, scope, and profitability increase as the businesses grow older, that the labor-intense mode of operation falls off sharply, and that, on the average, the firms become less highly leveraged.

Data on the life cycle characteristics of minority firms indicated that size and absolute profitability increase quite substantially as the firms grow older.

	Pre-1968 formations only	Post-1973 formations only
After-tax profits (median)	$40,856	$27,815
Annual sales (median)	1,045,170	554,577
Net worth (median)	193,900	74,995

On the positive side, discriminant analysis exercises that delineated younger firms from those formed prior to 1974 revealed that the former are earning a significantly higher rate of profit—15.8 percent (relative to total assets), compared to 13.9 percent for the older firms. Greater risk is apparently being incurred simultaneously with greater return.

Finally, the DFP data indicated that certain subsectors have very high levels of indebtedness relative to business equity. They are: black-owned firms; younger firms; and construction and wholesaling lines of business.

51. Timothy Bates. "Why Black Firms Fail." Chapter 3 in *Banking on Black Enterprise.* **Washington, D.C.: Joint Center for Political and Economic Studies, 1992 (forthcoming).**

• This study used the Characteristics of Business Owners (CBO) data base to investigate determinants of firm size and survival, focusing specifically on groups of black- and white-owned young firms (started between 1976 and 1982). Financial capital inputs at the point of business start-up were found to be the most important single determinant of differences in business viability among young firms. Mean values for financial capital inputs at start-up were as follows:

	Black firms	White firms
Equity capital	$9,054	$20,402
Debt capital	10,012	24,150
Total financial capital	19,066	44,552

Total financial capital input at start-up averaged $44,552 for whites, nearly two and one-half times greater than the mean financial capital input of $19,066 for blacks. The consequences of these huge differentials are profoundly important in explaining the generally laggard performance of black enterprise. The financial capital disparity is strongest in the case of debt, with mean debt among black firms amounting to only 41.5 percent of the $24,150 figure for white firms. Commercial banks were the main source of debt capital, exceeding by far the combined total of debt provided by all other sources.

A major finding of the analysis was that stronger business startups have greater access to financial capital; they are less likely to be undercapitalized relative to the weaker startup, which has severely limited access to financial capital sources such as commercial banks. Further, the greatest single disparity between the samples of young white and black firms was shown to lie in the financial capital structures of the two groups. White owners consistently commanded much more financial capital than black owners at the point of business entry: Differentials were widest for debt capital. In light of the findings linking the sales levels and survival prospects of black firms to the amount of financial capital invested, it is tempting to conclude that more debt causes healthier, larger scale business. This suggests that increasing the availability of debt would increase black business viability across-the-board. That may or may not be true. Before proceeding, it is useful to summarize what is known about those who enter business with large financial inputs.

- For both the black and white CBO business samples, debt and equity at the point of start-up were complements; that is, more of one was positively associated with more of the other, or the firms with the most debt were commonly those with the most equity.
- In these samples, the single most important determinant of debt level—for white as well as black firms—was the absolute size of equity capital inputs.
- Beyond equity, highly educated owners received the largest loans.
- A complementary study, Bates 1974 (see no. 15), showed that the owners receiving the largest loans possessed the highest personal incomes prior to entering small business.

The business owner with greater access to debt is therefore typically highly educated, has a high personal income, and invests a substantial amount of equity capital into the firm. All of this suggests the following two-stage line of causation:

1. High education
   High personal income   >   Large debt input in the
   High equity investment   small business
                                 start-up.

2. High education
   High personal income   >   Greater likelihood of
   High equity investment   small business viability.
   Large debt input

Would greater availability of loans help the weaker small businesses? It is important to recall that during the late 1960s and early 1970s, the Small Business Administration Economic Opportunity Loan program approved many thousands of loans to high-risk minority business borrowers who could not obtain loans from other sources. In their analysis of loan data from the Small Business Administration, Bates and Hester (1977; see no. 53b) showed that, other things equal, larger loans were directly associated with greater chances of failure. Greater access to debt is not a cure-all for minority business. The evidence indicates that, on balance, the stronger black-owned firms are the ones that are most likely to be handicapped by limited access to debt. Furthermore, limited credit access is most pronounced for firms that locate in minority communities. This phenomenon— redlining— is discussed in the review of "Small Business Viability in the Urban Ghetto" (no. 54).

52. Faith Ando. "Capital Issues and Minority-Owned Business." *The Review of Black Political Economy* 16 **(Spring 1988).**

• Ando demonstrated that after controlling for risk, established black-owned firms have substantially less success than nonminority firms in obtaining bank loans. The business samples used by Ando are not representative of the small business universe. Instead, the focus was on larger firms that were at least two years old in 1984. Roughly 80 percent of all firms in the United States in 1982 had zero employees; only 10 percent of the firms covered in Ando's study had zero employees. Among the black owners analyzed in this study, 84.0 percent had attended one or more years of college, compared to 79.0 percent of their nonminority cohorts. It is noteworthy that this elite group of black business owners experienced limited access to bank credit.

Ando's data focused on success in applying for bank loans over a three-year period in the early 1980s. The percentages of all short-term bank loan applications that were accepted were as follows:

Nonminorities	89.9
Asians	96.2
Blacks	61.7
Hispanics	86.6

The above figures do not necessarily reflect discrimination against blacks if, in fact, black loan applicants were higher credit risks overall than the others. To test for discrimination, therefore, Ando devised the following model of bank loan accessibility:

SUCCESS$_i$ = F(owner business experience, firm characteristics, loan terms, owner demographic characteristics)

where SUCCESS$_i$ is the success rate of the firm in applying for commercial bank loans. Ando found that when borrower credit risk is thusly controlled for, black businesses are significantly more likely to be denied access to commercial bank loans than nonminorities, Asians, or Hispanics. Ando explained success using a multiple linear regression model. The factors found to be most important for success in obtaining loans were:

- a large number of years of owner experience,
- large firm size,
- excellent credit rating, and
- request for short loan maturities.

The factors found to cause loan rejection were:
- a record of previous bankruptcy,
- a bad credit rating or lack of a credit rating,
- being in the wrong industry (e.g., manufacturing firms; the period under consideration coincided with widespread recession in manufacturing industries),
- divorced marital status of owner,
- needing cosigners because of insufficient collateral, and
- being black.

53a. Robert Edelstein. "Improving the Selection of Credit Risks: An Analysis of a Commercial Bank Minority Lending Program." *Journal of Finance* 30 (March 1975).

53b. Timothy Bates and Donald Hester. "Analysis of a Commercial Bank Minority Lending Program: Comment." *Journal of Finance* 32 (December 1977).

- A recurring controversy centers around the loan amounts extended to black-owned firms: Would larger loan amounts produce higher rates of survival? Robert Edelstein studied a sample of 290 black-owned firms that received loans from Philadelphia's Job Loan and Urban Venture Corporation between April 1968 and January 1970. All of the firms that received loans had previously had their loan applications rejected by commercial banks. Of the 290 borrowers, 42 percent were current in their loan repayment obligations in January 1970.

Edelstein concluded that loan repayment probability is higher for the black-owned firms receiving larger loans, receiving more recent loans, and whose owners have at least seven years of general employment experience. Edelstein criticized the Job Loan and Urban Venture Corporation for underfunding black business borrowers and hence increasing their probabilities of defaulting.

Bates and Hester cautioned that Edelstein's conclusion that "larger loans are positively related to superior loan repayment performance" (p. 44) is simplistic. Edelstein's conclusion could only be accepted if he had used a more extensive set of variables to measure the credit characteristics of loan applicants. Lenders clearly give larger loans to the more credit-worthy loan applicants. The issue that must be sorted out here can be stated simply: Does the strong loan applicant—a college graduate, for example—succeed in business because he or she got a large loan? Or is the large loan merely correlated to the fact that highly educated people tend to create viable, lasting small businesses? Edelstein's study was incapable of answering this question because he failed to control for the characteristics—such as education levels—that typify strong borrowers.

54. Timothy Bates. "Small Business Viability in the Urban Ghetto." *Journal of Regional Science* 29 (November 1989).

• The creation of viable small businesses commonly entails three elements: (1) talented and capable entrepreneurs who (2) have access to financial capital to invest in the business ventures and (3) access to markets for the products of their enterprises. The lack of one or more of these elements handicaps most small firms that operate in inner-city minority communities.

The relative performance of black- and nonminority-owned firms operating both inside and outside of urban minority residential areas was examined in this study. The healthier, emerging lines of black enterprise were shown to be shifting away from inner-city minority communities and focusing instead on central business districts or outlying suburban areas. One of the causes of this trend is that commercial banks are extensively redlining small firms that do business in minority areas. The net result is that better educated blacks are entering lines of business that are larger and more growth oriented, but that inner-city black communities are increasingly being left out of the business development process.

Usually, when someone borrows money from a commercial bank to establish a small business, the amount he or she receives depends first and foremost on the size of the equity investment that the owner is sinking into the new firm. The larger the equity investment, the greater the access to debt. The surest way to get a $100,000 bank loan to start up a business is to invest $50,000 or so of one's own money.

When blacks seek loans, the size of their equity investment is an important consideration in the eyes of commercial bankers in determining the amount to extend, but it is not typically the primary consideration. The primary consideration is the geographic location of the firm: if the proposed business is located in a minority community, then loan size is cut drastically.

In addition to analyzing loan size determination, this study analyzed data on young firms—those formed between 1976 and 1982—from the CBO data base to identify the factors that determine their prospects for survival. Discriminant analysis indicated that larger financial inputs at the point of business start-up are related positively to firm survival, irrespective of the race of the owner or the geographic location of the firm. Since owners with four or more years of college have greater access to debt capital, the firms that they form are larger and more viable, on average, than those started by their less educated cohorts. All of these findings suggest that development of the black business community would be fostered by the entry of highly educated owners who invest substantial amounts of financial capital in their firms. Among the black firms that were not located in the minority communities of large SMSAs, greater financial and human capital inputs are shown to be directly related to firm survival. For the firms that were still in business in late 1986, 37.9 percent of them served a predominantly minority clientele. Remaining in business was found to be associated with competing in the wider marketplace, which is why 62.1 percent of these black-owned firms were serving a clientele that was either racially diverse or largely nonminority.

If a major goal of minority business development is to aid economic development in minority communities, then something of a dilemma is posed by the fact that the group of black firms possessing the greatest development prospects is the one that is not located in the minority areas of large Standard Metropolitan Statistical Areas (SMSAs). Talented and capable minority entrepreneurs, access to capital, and access to markets—these were the ingredients identified with minority economic development. Among the black-owned firms not located in the large urban minority communities, this development formula applies directly: over half of the owners starting firms have attended college; the firms most likely to remain active are the ones started by owners with four or more years of college; the firms with larger financial capital inputs and racially diverse clienteles are most likely to remain in business.

Within the minority communities, in contrast, capital access is constrained and the black business start-ups that survive consist disproportionately of tiny firms serving minority clienteles. Remaining in business in this milieu is directly associated with minimal owner education: high school dropouts who often hang on by running small firms such as beauty parlors and that typically have no paid employees and minimal prospects for alleviating ghetto economic underdevelopment. It appears likely that many of these firms may be incapable of competing in the broader marketplace. Unless greater financial capital is forthcoming and better educated owners are induced to remain in business, the black business community in the minority neighborhoods of large urban areas is destined to stagnate.

55. Gavin Chen and John Cole. "The Myths, Facts, and Theories of Ethnic Small-Scale Enterprise Financing." *The Review of Black Political Economy* **16 (Spring 1988).**

• The authors reviewed various studies of capital issues affecting minority business development, and they examined selected small business information drawn from the CBO data base. They concluded that all small businesses face "crowding out" phenomena in accessing conventional capital markets. Relative to large firms, capital is less available and more expensive. Nonetheless, all minorities do not face the same sorts of barriers regarding access to capital, cost of capital, and credit discrimination: Blacks experience greater difficulties than Asians and Hispanics. Black-owned firms are undercapitalized compared to others because of relatively low owner equity investment from personal assets, low community input to firm equity, low community response to firm debt investment, and credit discrimination by commercial financial institutions.

Chen and Cole concluded that the nomenclature "minority" as a broad category is a misnomer in the case of business development. Hypotheses regarding differences in access to capital, use of capital, and cost of capital between minority and nonminority firms are generally supported empirically. "However, when the data are further disaggregated to show the major ethnic components of the minority category, dissimilarities among the minority groups and similarities to the nonminority groups appear" (p.121).

Editorial note: Chen and Cole treated "Hispanic" as one category. Yet disaggregation of Hispanics into groups of Cubans, Mexicans, and so forth would have further reinforced their point about dissimilarities among minority groups. Specifically, Mexican-Americans have less access to financial capital than other Hispanic groups such as Cubans.

Structural Barriers to Small Business Entry

There is very little concrete evidence on why minorities choose to concentrate heavily in certain industry groups such as services or retailing. Three pioneering studies of this topic are reviewed in this section. Since severe data inadequacies handicap this line of research, the findings of these studies must be viewed as suggestive and preliminary.

Roger Waldinger (no. 56) identified numerous market conditions that encourage entry into small business, but he offered no statistical evidence to support his insightful analysis. Studies by Arthur Woolf (no. 57) and by Margaret Simms and Lynn Burbridge (no. 58) examined statistical evidence on industry characteristics that influence which sectors attract minority-owned businesses.

56. Roger Waldinger. *Through the Eye of the Needle: Immigrants and Enterprise in New York's Garment Trades.* New York: New York University Press, 1986.

• An environment favorable to small minority-owned firms is one in which the market is too small or too differentiated to support mass production or distribution. Ethnic consumer tastes, for example, often create small market niches that major retail chains overlook. The retail giants minimize costs by doing large volumes of business in a few basic product lines and centralizing administrative functions. Thus, the chain stores may be unwilling to stock the specialty items that are demanded by a nearby Jamaican neighborhood but not by the nearby Dominican area. In the case of immigrant groups, large stores may have limited information about specific tastes and wants. In this case, co-ethnics may operate small firms catering to specific tastes. The market niche that results may be reinforced if immigrant consumers prefer to deal with co-ethnic merchants.

Low capital-to-labor ratios provide easy entry into many lines of business, a condition that is likely to favor the creation of minority firms. Labor-intensive production processes combined with small markets that inhibit economies of scale allow minority firms to operate efficiently despite their typically small scale of operations. Unstable product demand also reinforces the advantages to small firms, since it may endanger investment in fixed plants and equipment. When demand in a particular industry falls into stable and unstable portions, the industry is often segmented into two branches: the larger firms handle the stable products, and the smaller firms cater to the unpredictable or fluctuating portion. Minority business is invariably more widespread in the unstable industry sector.

Low technical barriers to entry are often an inducement to create small firms. Taxi driving, for example, utilizes a skill that is widespread in the labor force. Economies of large scale production are lacking in this industry, and fixed-cost reductions can be realized by working long hours. Owner-operators amenable to self-exploitation can achieve reductions in fixed costs by working very long hours behind the wheel of a cab. Trucking, another popular line of minority enterprise, is similarly suited for the minority entrepreneur who is willing to work long hours.

Many of the market conditions favoring small business—low capital-to-labor ratios, unstable product demand, and small markets—characterize the urban garment industry. In urban fashion market centers where minority immigrant firms are concentrated, the average number of workers per establishment is low: 21 in Miami, 26 in Los Angeles, and 29 in New York. Barriers to entry are low: "for as little as $25,000 a neophyte garment capitalist can purchase a 25-30 person factory, complete with a boiler to generate steam. Moreover, dealers provide generous financing terms: a down payment of $6,000-$7,000 usually suffices" (pp. 137-38). The starting points for such garment firms are the low-priced, style-oriented product lines where volatility keeps barriers to entry low. In New York's Chinatown, Chinese garment manufacturers grew in number from eight in 1960 to 480 in 1985: "20,000 Chinese workers—more than one-sixth of the city's entire apparel labor force—were employed in Chinese-owned concerns" (p. 3).

57. Arthur Woolf. "Market Structure and Minority Presence: Black-Owned Firms in Manufacturing." *The Review of Black Political Economy* **14 (Spring 1986).**

• The barriers that prevent small firms from entering a given industry sector are critical determinants of the presence of black-owned firms. The Survey of Minority-Owned Business Enterprise (SMOBE) data indicate that only 2 percent of all black businesses were in manufacturing in the 1970s, but that 2 percent accounted for 7.5 percent of the sales volume of all black-owned firms. Furthermore, in the industry groups in which black manufacturers are located, nearly 70 percent of the total labor force consists of blue-collar workers. Expansion in these lines of manufacturing, therefore, is likely to create the types of jobs that are readily accessible to unemployed minority workers.

An analysis of black manufacturing firms that use paid employees reveals several statistically significant patterns of concentration. The firms are heavily concentrated in fields that are dominated by small businesses (those having annual sales under $5 million). They are overrepresented in the slow growth and no growth fields—the lines of manufacturing that are laggard overall. They are less prevalent in fields where advertising is used extensively, suggesting that industry orientation toward product advertising is an entry barrier for black firms. The fact that suitable data were available for only 45 lines of manufacturing somewhat limits the ability to generalize these findings. Finally, black-owned manufacturing firms were somewhat more likely to operate in fields where government purchases a large share of industry output, but this relationship was statistically insignificant.

58. Margaret Simms and Lynn Burbridge. *Minority Business Formation and Failure by Industry and by Location.* **Washington, D.C.: U.S. Department of Commerce, Minority Business Development Agency, 1986.**

• This study examines the industry characteristics that influence which sectors minority entrepreneurs enter, as well as whether or not they succeed in those sectors. Most minority businesses are small, and small businesses tend to concentrate heavily in certain industry sectors. For minorities overall, empirical analysis confirmed the conventional wisdom that minorities tend to enter growth industries but not capital-intensive industries. Growth, however, appears to be a better predictor of entry for blacks, whereas capital intensity is a better predictor for Hispanics and Asians. The small impact of capital intensity for blacks was an unexpected, puzzling finding.

The lack of consistent data across all industries partially frustrated the authors in their efforts to study the impacts of various indices upon industry structure. Missing variables necessitated dropping certain industries, leaving a sample of 45 industries for analysis.

Minority business failure rates were found to be higher in communities with slow economic growth. Failure rates tended to be lower in communities where large proportions of the population were minority, but "the richer that minority population is, the more likely minority businesses are to fail" (p. iv). In light of this negative relationship between minority income levels and minority business survival rates, reliance on minority customers alone is possibly not a prudent business marketing strategy.

Access to Markets, Job Creation, and Related Issues

Minority-owned firms rely heavily on the minority community as a market for their goods and services. Traditional lines of business—personal services and small-scale retailing—rely more than others on the minority market. "The Urban Ghetto Milieu" (no. 60) shows that firms, whether white- or black-owned, catering to the minority marketplace tend to be smaller and more failure-prone than those competing in the nonminority marketplace. The rapid growth industries for black-owned business are those that cater to a clientele that is either racially mixed or largely nonminority, such as business

71

services.   The negative effect of resource flows on the operating environs of low-income, inner-city minority communities is discussed in the study by Bates and Daniel Fusfeld (no. 62) and the study by Richard Schaffer (no. 63). The ghetto economy tends to produce weak internal markets as well as capital flight, and educated people tend to be drained away from it. More attractive markets, according to a study by Bates (no. 64), are likely to be found in the growth of set-asides and procurement efforts targeted at minority businesses.   Yet these programs must adapt to new judicial standards if they are to survive at the state and local government levels.

In two other studies (nos. 65 and 66), Bates examined the job creation patterns among black- and white-owned small businesses that operate in large metropolitan areas. The findings show that the labor force of black-owned firms is largely minority, whereas the labor force of white-owned firms consists mostly of nonminorities. Even among the nonminority firms that operate in minority communities, most of the employees are white. Black business expansion, irrespective of firm location, tends to create jobs for minorities.

59. John Handy and David Swinton. "The Determinants of the Rate of Growth of Black-Owned Businesses." *The Review of Black Political Economy* **12 (Spring 1984).**

• Black firms frequently sell to other minorities, and this is particularly true of those located in the minority communities of the nation's largest metropolitan areas.   Findings by Handy and Swinton indicated that the local black clientele is still an overwhelmingly important market for black-owned firms. They found that growth in black business receipts between 1972 and 1977 was powerfully influenced by the strength of local black purchasing power.

60. Timothy Bates. "The Urban Ghetto Milieu." Chapter 4 in *Banking on Black Enterprise.* **Washington, D.C.: Joint Center for Political and Economic Studies, 1992 (forthcoming).**

• The characteristics of many urban minority communities are low and variable personal incomes, low labor force participation rates, and high unemployment rates. They are poverty ghettos. And the state of the ghetto business community reflects the fact that the internal market is weak due to the low incomes of most of its residents. Information from the Characteristics of Business Owners (CBO) data base indicates that both black and white firms differ systematically in terms of sales, employment, and discontinuance rates when they are divided into two groups: (1) those serving clienteles that are largely or entirely minority and (2) those serving clienteles that are either racially diverse or largely nonminority. The firms described below were classified as minority-market oriented if 75 percent or more of their customers were minorities; the others were classified as nonminority-marketplace oriented. White-owned firms that are minority-market oriented actually have higher discontinuance rates than black minority-market firms.

Firms oriented toward the minority marketplace (mean values):

	Black firms	White male firms
1982 sales	$49,362	$96,501
No. of employees	0.6	1.0
Percent still active, 1986	73.5%	69.8%

Firms competing in the nonminority marketplace (mean values):

	Black firms	White male firms
1982 sales	$70,211	$174,593
No. of employees	1.0	2.1
Percent still active, 1986	74.7%	79.0%

All of the firms described above were operating in 28 large metropolitan areas in 1982. Among black firms doing business in these areas, personal service firms relied the most on the minority market; construction firms relied the least on minority clienteles. The clienteles of the majority of black firms in three industry groups—construction, manufacturing, and business services—are either racially diverse or largely nonminority. Fewer than 15 percent of the personal service firms, in contrast, compete in the nonminority marketplace. Traditional lines of black enterprise—typified by the personal services—are largely small, ghetto-based firms that serve minority customers. After personal services, the line of black business that relies most heavily on minority clienteles is retailing.

For professionals as well as high school dropouts, black self-employment in the minority market sector is associated with very small firms, high rates of business discontinuance, and minimal growth potential.

61. Timothy Bates. "Urban Economic Transformation and Minority Business Opportunities." *The Review of Black Political Economy* **13 (Winter 1984-1985).**

• This study hypothesized that major structural changes in urban areas were key determinants of minority business markets. Specifically, large, older central cities are rapidly being transformed into areas where administrative and service functions are the dominant economic activities. The growth of corporate and government administrative activities in the business districts of central cities created a need for complementary activities, especially services to businesses. Corporate headquarters, for example, are major purchasers of the following services: advertising, accounting, legal, temporary secretarial, maintenance, and computer. Small firms that offer business services are thriving in the big cities, and black-owned firms have been a major beneficiary of the trend. Employment in business service firms owned by blacks grew by 56.8 percent between 1972 and 1977, and the number of firms in this field increased by 47.6 percent.

62. Timothy Bates and Daniel Fusfeld. "The Economic Dynamics of the Urban Ghetto." Chapter 10 in *The Political Economy of the Urban Ghetto.* **Carbondale, IL: Southern Illinois University Press, 1984.**

• Poverty ghettos in urban areas are depressed enclaves within a prosperous economy: Income, resources, and people interact with poverty and underdevelopment in a system of cumulative causation that maintains the ghetto as a characteristic feature of the national economy. The patterns of the ghetto economy reinforce themselves—poverty reinforces the conditions that lead to poverty; resources that might lead to economic development are drained out.

The chief resource of the economy in the ghetto is labor, and the largest flow of income comes from employment. In most ghettos, a substantial minority of the labor force is employed in middle-income jobs; few attain high wage employment. The higher income residents are the ones who are most likely to move out.

Income flows out of the ghetto in much the same way as capital and labor. Ghetto residents buy goods produced elsewhere in stores that are typically owned by outsiders. Internal flows of income that might support greater economic activity and higher incomes within the ghetto are largely absent. Rather, ghetto income supports economic activity elsewhere.

The ownership of rental housing by community residents, when it does happen, rechannels purchasing power back into the local economy, with attendant multiplier effects (for a definition of multiplier effects, see Appendix C). Yet ghetto rental housing is owned overwhelmingly by outsiders, and the monthly rent checks do not come back into the ghetto to support other enterprises or employees.

Capital also flows out of ghettos through the deterioration of public facilities. Fiscally strapped older cities have a universal tendency to maintain facilities in middle- and upper-income areas and to put the needs of the ghetto last. Schools, libraries, and medical facilities deteriorate, parks become run down, streets and curbs go unrepaired.

Financial institutions have traditionally done a minimal job of servicing the loan demands of ghetto households and businesses. A substantial portion of the savings of the urban ghetto goes into banks and savings and loan associations (S&Ls) whose investment policies draw funds out of the area and into business loans, mortgages, and other investments elsewhere. Little comes back to support the ghetto economy or to promote its development.

Development of financial institutions such as banks, S&Ls, and credit unions typically stimulates economic growth by mobilizing savings that residents would otherwise hold as idle cash balances. Households and businesses depend on the availability of funds from financial institutions to finance economic activities beyond those supportable by their internal capacity to raise funds. The mere existence of financial institutions, however, provides no assurance that development will increase in ghetto areas. Local savers may enjoy the benefits of safety and convenience that financial institutions provide, but local borrowers may not gain access to the pool of savings that the banks and S&Ls assemble.

75

The drain on resources, therefore, tends to undermine economic development in the ghetto. Income flows rarely strengthen and support savings, housing, or the infrastructure; rather, they tend to drain out quickly, supporting economic activity located elsewhere.

The most serious drainage, however, has come from labor, and it has intensified in recent years. The ghetto's chief resource is labor, and its best products have increasingly been departing by way of the educational system and the high-wage economy. Many of the most intelligent, capable, and imaginative young people have been drawn into the economic mainstream, where the rewards are greater and the opportunities wider than those in the urban poverty areas. The best and brightest are drawn out of the ghetto to serve themselves and the dominant society. Programs that enable some to escape the ghetto, therefore, preserve and reinforce ghettoization for many more.

By way of summary, Bates and Fusfeld describe a ghetto economy whose poverty is partially maintained by:

- outflows of capital in several forms—savings, housing, and infrastructure;
- outflows of incomes exacerbated by weak internal income flows and a low resultant regional multiplier; and
- outflows of many intelligent, capable, and imaginative young people by way of the educational system and the high-wage economy.

Stripped of capital and entrepreneurial talent, the ghetto really has no prospect of generating the internal economic development it needs to produce jobs and incomes for its residents. Creating and expanding black-owned businesses and financial institutions could reverse all of the outflows described above, but such an approach is fraught with risks due to lack of capital, weak markets, and related factors.

63. Richard Schaffer. *Income Flows in Urban Poverty Areas: A Comparison of the Community Income Accounts of Bedford-Stuyvesant and Borough Park.* Lexington, Mass.: Lexington Books, 1973.

- In any community, the goods purchased are largely imported, and in this respect, ghettos are like any other urban area. In most communities, however, a significant portion of the retail and wholesale establishments are owned locally, and the incomes of the owners are largely spent locally. A chain of spending and respending is set up which adds strength and variety to the local economy.

In his study of the income flows of Bedford-Stuyvesant, Schaffer estimated that resident owners of businesses in the community received $400,000 in profits from local businesses. Nonresident owners, in contrast, received profits of $14.1 million. In other words, most of the business profits generated accrue to nonresident owners and, therefore, most of the profit flows out of the community.

Probably the greatest amount of capital flows out of the ghetto through rental housing. Minimal maintenance of facilities allows landlords to withdraw their capital from real estate investments. Landlords withdrew $25.8 million in Bedford-Stuyvesant in 1969, according to Schaffer. With wear and tear the property will ultimately be worthless, but as it is being used up owners can realize positive cash flows while they take out their capital. And their failure to maintain property structures causes surrounding owners to do likewise as a matter of self-protection. One deteriorated building draws down the value of surrounding property.

64. Timothy Bates. "Public Policy That Would Make A Difference." Chapter 7 In _Banking on Black Enterprise_. Washington, D.C.: Joint Center for Political and Economic Studies, 1992 (forthcoming).

• The most noteworthy change for black firms in the realm of market access has come about through the growth of set-asides and procurement efforts targeted specifically at minorities. Large corporations in consumer products industries have targeted procurement dollars to minority firms. Government set-asides for minorities constitute a multibillion dollar market. Federal government agencies have also subsidized private groups, such as the National Minority Supplier Development Council, which in turn have encouraged minority business set-aside programs throughout the corporate sector. The rise of black political power at the local level has been a powerful impetus to the expansion of minority set-asides. The superior performance of emerging black firms in large urban areas with black mayors presiding reflects the success of these preferential procurement efforts. Yet, the programs must adapt to new judicial standards if they are to survive at the state and local government levels.

On April 11, 1982, the city council of Richmond, Virginia, adopted a minority business set-aside plan that required recipients of city-awarded construction contracts to subcontract at least 30 percent of each contract to minority-owned firms. Richmond argued that the plan attempted to remedy various forms of past discrimination that were responsible for the small number of local minority construction firms. As an example, the city cited the exclusion of blacks from skilled construction trade unions and training programs.

In a 1989 Supreme Court decision, *City of Richmond* v. *J.A. Croson Co.*, Justice Sandra Day O'Connor rejected this argument as "an amorphous claim." According to O'Connor, "a generalized assertion that there has been past discrimination in an entire industry provides no guidance for a legislative body to determine the precise scope of the injury it seeks to remedy." Justice O'Connor did, however, indicate that minority business set-aside programs may be acceptable, despite the Court's negative ruling: "Nothing we say today precludes a state or local entity from taking action to rectify the effects of identified discrimination within its jurisdiction." Furthermore, she stated, "evidence of a pattern of individual discriminatory acts can, if supported by *appropriate statistical proof,* lend support to a local government's determination that broader remedial relief is justified" (*Richmond* v. *Croson*; emphasis added). Finally, where there is a significant statistical disparity between the number of qualified minority contractors willing and able to perform a particular service and the number of subcontractors actually engaged by the locality or the locality's prime contractors, discriminatory exclusion could be inferred.

In reality, large cities and states should be able to statistically demonstrate disparities between the minority business share of city and state contracts and the number of minority firms that are willing and able to undertake such work. For example, if minority contractors made up 8 percent of all contractors in the state of Maryland but had been awarded only 2 percent of the dollar amount of state construction contracts during the past decade, then the state of Maryland could legally adopt a goal of increasing the share of contracts targeted to minority firms. It would be a straightforward matter for Maryland to select random samples of several hundred minority and nonminority contractors. The samples could then be surveyed to establish scientifically the proportions of minority and nonminority contractors that were "willing and able" to work for the state.

Another justification for minority set-asides that would likely meet the Supreme Court's standard of strict scrutiny involves the "passive participant" doctrine. According to Justice O'Connor, "Any public entity, state or federal, has a compelling interest in assuring that public dollars. . . do not serve to finance the evil of private prejudice. . . . if the city could show that it had essentially become a 'passive participant' in a system of racial exclusion. . . the city could take affirmative steps to dismantle such a system" (*Richmond* v. *Croson*).

Bates ("Small Business Viability in the Urban Ghetto"; see no. 54) has documented that commercial banks redline black-owned firms that operate in urban minority communities. This discrimination in lending reduces the viability of black firms, which in turn lessens their ability to compete for procurement contracts. A set-aside program that sought to assist firms operating in redlined areas would be able to cite the "passive participant" doctrine to justify its actions. Similarly, Ando ("Capital Issues and Minority-Owned Business"; see no. 52) has shown that black firms are significantly less likely than others to have their bank loan applications approved.

In the future, minority business set-asides may no longer be referred to explicitly as minority business set-aside programs. Instead, set-aside procurement regulations might refer to "disadvantaged" businesses, and procurement officials will have broad discretionary powers in deciding which firms qualify as disadvantaged.

Flexible procurement programs that put forth goals for helping disadvantaged businesses, of course, can be effective minority business set-aside programs only if they are administered by procurement officials that truly want to help minority-owned firms. Vague wording of set-aside regulations necessarily puts great discretionary power into the hands of those who administer the programs. The political will to make minority set-asides work effectively has always been key to their success and it is vital to the future of minority business set-aside programs.

65. Timothy Bates. "Do Black-Owned Businesses Employ Minority Workers? New Evidence." *The Review of Black Political Economy* **16 (Spring 1988).**

• Most of the workers employed by black-owned firms are minorities, according to this study of

CBO data on small businesses. This employment pattern is typical of small as well as large black-owned firms and of firms in blue-collar industries such as construction as well as white-collar industries such as finance. A comparison of the employment patterns of black- and white-owned small firms is revealing: minorities comprise 50 percent or more of the workers in 86.0 percent of black-owned firms and 18.3 percent of white-owned firms. In fact, for 78.8 percent of black employers, 75 percent or more of the paid workers are minorities.

At the other end of the spectrum, 4.6 percent of black-owned firms and 61.2 percent of white-owned firms have no minority employees.

The hypothesis that relying on minority workers may restrict the viability of black firms was tested statistically and rejected. There appears to be no relationship between firm viability and the racial composition of the labor force.

66. Timothy Bates. "Firm Location and Bank Redlining." Chapter 5 in *Banking on Black Enterprise*. Washington, D.C.: Joint Center for Political and Economic Studies, 1992 (forthcoming).

• The small business employment patterns described in the study above (no. 65) indicated that 61.2 percent of white small business employers have no minority employees. A possible reason for this high rate is that some firms are located in areas where minorities do not commonly reside. This study, in contrast, looked solely at the employment patterns of small firms operating in 28 large metropolitan areas, all of which have substantial minority populations. Looking solely at firms operating in urban minority communities, the data indicated that nearly one-third of the white small business employers have no minority workers on their payrolls.

Employers in minority communities	Black firms	White firms
Percentage with no minority employees	1.9%	32.9%
Percentage with 50 percent or more minority employees	96.2	37.6

In complete contrast, nearly all of the black firms had minority employees: 93.1 percent of the black employers relied on minority workers for at least 75 percent of their employees.

Within the same 28 large metropolitan areas, small business employers operating in nonminority areas (including nonresidential areas) were examined. Among the black employers, 86.7 percent had work forces made up of 50 percent or more minorities; most of them relied on minority employees for over 75 percent of their work force.

Employers in nonminority areas	Black firms	White firms
No minority employees	3.1%	62.7%
50 percent or more minority employees	86.7	20.4

Among the white-owned small businesses in the same areas, most had no minority employees whatsoever. The prevalence of minority employees typifies large and small black firms, white-collar industries such as finance and insurance, and blue-collar industries such as manufacturing and construction. Among the white firms, minority employment was widespread only in the manufacturing and construction industries.

For the entire 28 metropolitan areas—minority as well as nonminority sections—57.8 percent of the white small business employers had no minority workers at all, and 17.8 percent of them employed minorities for 75 percent or more of their total employment. The corresponding figures for the black firms were 2.2 percent and 89.0 percent, respectively. The expansion of black business tends to create jobs for minorities, irrespective of whether the expanding firms are located in minority communities.

The Impact of Black Elected Officials on Black Business Development

67. Gerald Jaynes and Robin Williams, editors. *A Common Destiny: Blacks in American Society*. Washington, D.C.: National Academy Press, 1989.

• The evidence that is available on this important topic indicates that black mayors place a high priority on minority business development. This commitment translates into larger and more successful black-owned businesses in areas with black mayors presiding.

Evidence from case studies indicated that black mayors place a high priority on municipal contracting with minority-owned businesses. Indeed, promoting black-owned businesses was ranked as "very important" by 86 percent of black elected officials (p. 250). As of 1990, however, no studies had examined the impact of the policies of black mayors on the overall health of minority business.

68. Timothy Bates. "Black Mayors and the Impact of Set-Asides." Chapter 6 in *Banking on Black Enterprise.* **Washington, D.C.: Joint Center for Political and Economic Studies, 1992 (forthcoming).**

• This study compared the performance of emerging lines of black business in two types of urban areas: those that have black mayors and those that do not. The findings indicated that the presence of a black mayor is associated with a black business community of larger firms, more employees, and lower business failure rates. Progress is most apparent among the younger firms. The larger emerging lines of black enterprise that benefit most directly from minority business set-asides and preferential procurement programs flourish in the environs where black mayors preside.

Two sequential events promoted the growth of procurement opportunities for black-owned firms in these urban areas: first, the election of a black mayor, and second, the appointment of appropriate officials who promoted preferential procurement programs for minority enterprise. The opportunities that resulted then lured potential entrepreneurs into self-employment. Most of those who created firms were college graduates, and they made large financial capital investments in the businesses that they established. The fact that a disproportionately larger number of substantive black businesses are emerging and successfully entering the market for procurement contracts in the urban areas with black mayors presiding suggests that black political power creates business opportunities (and not the other way around).

However, it appears that a majority of black-owned firms do not benefit directly from procurement programs targeted to minorities. In all of the relevant large metropolitan areas, the most common line of business start-up for black entrepreneurs in the 1976-1982 period was small-scale retailing; by 1986, 40.6 percent of these retail operations had closed down. This high rate of business discontinuance was typical of the firms in metropolitan areas with black mayors as well as the firms in other urban areas. Policy choices made in the mayor's office probably had little relevance for the fate of these black-owned retail ventures. It is the emerging lines of black enterprise—wholesaling, construction, business services, etc.—that are most capable of benefiting from procurement efforts. These are the types of business that are prospering in the urban areas with black mayors.

Asian and Hispanic Self-Employment

Sociologists conducted most of the studies summarized in this section. Sociological studies of minority entrepreneurship have most commonly focused on groups of immigrants, particularly recent immigrants to the United States. These studies rarely use sophisticated statistical methodology to sort out and pin down cause and effect relationships between individual or group traits and business success. For example, the study by Edna Bonacich and Ivan Light (no. 73) noted that recent Korean immigrants effectively used family resources such as unpaid labor to develop successful businesses. These Korean immigrants, however, also tended to be highly educated persons with white-collar work experience, and many of them possessed substantial financial capital. It is thus difficult to identify the relative importance of the numerous attributes of Korean entrepreneurs that are responsible for success in small business.

When sociologists discard statistical proof as a methodological tool, they free themselves to speculate on the less tangible determinants of small business success. The studies tend to be provocative and interesting, even though they produce little in the way of hard evidence about the causes of minority business performance. The last study in this section (no. 75), by Development Associates, Inc., is an exception to this rule: It relied heavily on statistical analysis of data that were systematically compiled. This study of young adults and their inclinations toward self-employment found that young blacks exhibit a greater inclination toward small business ownership than any other minority (or nonminority) group. In light of the fact that blacks have the lowest actual rate of self-employment among the groups studied, this finding highlights an essential element of entrepreneurial reality:

Inclinations can be translated into viable business operations only when one possesses both the relevant skills and the financial resources that make up the price of admission to the world of business ownership.

69. Ivan Light. *Ethnic Enterprise in America*. Berkeley: University of California Press, 1972.

• Light employed a wealth of secondary information in his historical, sociological investigation of self-employment among Chinese, Japanese, and black Americans. Ethnic resources are highlighted as key reasons for the greater success of Chinese and Japanese small businesses relative to black businesses. The ethnic resources that assist business formation and operation include cultural endowments and solidarities. One important manifestation of these resources, particularly among first generation Chinese and Japanese, was the rotating credit association. Capital access constraints on small business formation were overcome by these associations, which were operated by groups of close associates. Each member of the rotating credit association made regular cash contributions, thereby creating a pool of savings that members could borrow for such purposes as forming a small business. There is no evidence that blacks in the United States have created similar associations.

Other ethnic resources used by Chinese and Japanese in America included support groups based on kinship, old-country residence, and trade employment. Group members provided assistance to fellow villagers, kin, and tradesmen who sought to operate their own businesses. Seldom did immigrants enter into self-employment without the aid of these social support networks.

Similar social support networks were sometimes created in black communities through social ties in churches, fraternal orders, and lodges. Insurance companies, for example, evolved from the benefit coverage initially provided by black mutual-aid societies. Similarly, black religious movements—the Father Divine Peace Mission, for example—spawned some small business development. But these support networks were less comprehensive than the extensive Chinese and Japanese social support networks, which created more extensive community-based business opportunities.

70. Roger Waldinger.
Through the Eye of the
Needle: Immigrants and
Enterprise in New York's
Garment Trades. **New York:**
New York University Press,
1986.

• Waldinger's analysis of immigrant-owned firms in the New York City garment industry focused on minority-owned business. Much of it was based on a survey of 136 garment firms, 63 of them owned by Chinese, and 32 owned by Dominicans. His complex theory of immigrant enterprise applies to disadvantaged groups in general, and can be applied to a wide range of industries. It is therefore truly a theory of minority enterprise, despite its narrow empirical base on garment firms owned by Chinese and Dominicans.

According to Waldinger, opportunities for small business ownership result often from the process of ethnic succession. Natives gradually opt out of certain industries for a variety of interrelated reasons: (1) low economic returns relative to alternatives, (2) uncertain economic rewards, (3) long hours, (4) low status of small business operation. Ethnic succession often stretches across several generations. A 1981 survey of the Jewish population in New York reported "consistently declining rates of self-employment from first generation to third, with much higher levels of education in the latter generation suggesting that much of its self-employment was concentrated in the professions rather than in business" (p. 28).

Among white ethnic owners of larger small businesses in the New York area (sales up to $5 million), however, a 1983 survey reported that only a fifth of the owners wanted their children to go into the family business. In the larger, more profitable fields, parents are much more likely to want to keep the business in the family—that is, to turn it over to their children. Ethnic succession is most pronounced in the smaller, low-profit fields, because the children don't want to succeed their parents in such firms. Thus, small grocery stores in New York City have passed from Jewish to Italian to Korean ownership; wholesalers, in contrast, continue to be the domain of white ethnics.

Minorities have become dominant in New York City garment contracting fields because of the opportunities created by ethnic succession. Vacancies are created as the previously dominant groups move up the socioeconomic ladder. But why have Chinese and Dominican entrepreneurs chosen to be the replacement groups?

Waldinger stressed blocked mobility as a key stimulus to self-employment. Impediments to stable salaried employment—poor English-language ability, inadequate or inappropriate skills, discrimination—lead many to pursue self-employment. In addition to constrained alternatives, Chinese and Dominican immigrants have access to certain ethnic resources that make self-employment advantageous. They draw upon family labor and the labor of co-ethnics, as well as a shared set of "understandings about the appropriate behavior and expectations within the work setting" (p. 46). A loyal, hard working labor force is often acquired at low cost: "Recruiting through kin and friendship networks promoted a paternalistic relationship between immigrant owners and their employees" (p. 159).

Most of the immigrant Chinese and Dominican owners surveyed by Waldinger were operating firms that were essentially way stations for new arrivals. Owners typically helped workers with the problems of adjustment to a new society. For example, they provided short-term loans to help employees obtain rental housing. Waldinger stressed that one of the comparative advantages to the immigrant garment firms in New York City is the loyal work force of family members and friendship networks. According to one Chinese owner, "Relatives are a must. You need people to take care of all departments, and when you start out you don't have enough money to hire as many people as you need" (p. 157).

One type of ethnic resource that was not important among the immigrant garment firms was the rotating credit association. These associations were credited (Light, 1972; see no. 69) as a major aid to small business entry among Asians. Yet Waldinger reports that "the emergence of immigrant-owned garment firms owes little to the role of ethnic credit-raising associations. . . only two of the Chinese firms attributed any assistance to family associations or rotating credit associations" (p. 136). Business start-ups were most commonly financed by personal savings, loans from commercial banks, family, and friends.

One unexpected finding of Waldinger's survey was the starkly different attitudes towards self-employment expressed by Dominicans and Chinese. Dominican garment entrepreneurs commonly expressed variants of the American Dream: Work hard and success will follow; self-employment is the best way to get ahead in the U.S. Not one Dominican mentioned discrimination as a barrier to advancement. In contrast, most Chinese felt that self-employment was not the best way to get ahead in U.S. society. The key to success, rather, was to graduate from college and to work for a large corporation. Most of them would prefer to work for large, stable firms but felt they lacked the appropriate linguistic and technical skills. In complete contrast to the Dominicans, many Chinese complained of being constrained—by language, lack of capital, and especially, discrimination.

The differing backgrounds of Dominican and Chinese garment entrepreneurs prior to immigration undoubtedly account for their different attitudes toward self-employment. Most of the Dominicans came from poor rural areas, and their educational backgrounds were weak. Relative to home, the opportunities in New York City seemed expansive. Self-employment was seen as a preferable alternative to low wage, dead-end service or factory jobs. The backgrounds of the Chinese were entirely different. They were much better educated, and many had been white-collar workers in large urban areas before migrating. The perception of relative disadvantage was strongest among the younger, better educated Chinese owners, many of whom felt that their status in New York City was worse than it had been at home. Thus, the key differences between Chinese and Dominican owners are rooted largely in class background rather than race or ethnicity.

71. Timothy Bates. "The Changing Nature of Minority Business: A Comparative Analysis of Asian, Non-minority, and Black-Owned Businesses." *The Review of Black Political Economy* **18 (Fall 1989).**

• This study utilized the Characteristics of Business Owners (CBO) database to compare the performances of small businesses formed between 1976 and 1982 by three groups: (1) Asian males, (2) black males, and (3) nonminority males. Labels such as "disadvantaged minority" simply cannot be applied overall to the community of Asian-owned businesses that existed in the United States in the 1980s. A comparison of the firms started by Asian and nonminority males between 1976 and 1982 was particularly revealing.

• 58.8 percent of the Asians entering self-employment had attended four or more years of college, versus 35.3 percent of the nonminorities.

- The business discontinuance (failure) rate, as of 1986, was 19.8 percent higher for the nonminorities.
- Mean owner financial capital investment at the point of start-up was $57,700 for the Asian firms, compared to $44,600 for the nonminority firms.
- The lines of small business in which profitability is highest— professional services, wholesaling, and finance, insurance, and real estate—accounted for 28.5 percent of the Asian business start-ups, compared to 23.1 percent of the nonminority business formations.

Even in the line of business where mean profitability is lowest for Asian males (retailing), they still out-performed nonminority males operating in this field. From a policy standpoint, Asians are not a disadvantaged group; thus, their eligibility for minority business set-asides, financial assistance, and so forth is inappropriate.

The status of black-owned firms is entirely different. A comparison of businesses started between 1976 and 1982 by black and nonminority males highlights some of the barriers to black enterprise viability.

- 21.7 percent of the black males entering self-employment were high school dropouts, compared to 11.3 percent of the nonminority males.
- Median and mean values for financial capital investment at start-up for blacks was less than half of the corresponding values reported by nonminorities.
- Blacks were overrepresented in lines of business that have below average profitability, as well as those with above average failure rates, relative to whites.

72. Edna Bonacich and John Modell. *The Economic Basis of Ethnic Solidarity: Small Business in the Japanese American Community.* Berkeley: University of California Press, 1980.

- Japanese residing in the western region of the United States were very heavily concentrated in several lines of small business prior to World War II: personal services, small-scale retailing, and farming. Los Angeles in1941 was typical: 47 percent of the employed Japanese males were self-employed. Among those over age 45, the incidence of self-employment exceeded 60 percent. Family members often worked unpaid in the small businesses.

Why the high degree of self-employment? Furthermore, why did it decline rapidly after World War II? Blocked mobility explained much of the concentration in self-employment. Intense racism directed at West Coast Japanese before and during World War II choked off opportunities for advancement in the general economy, thereby forcing many of them to work in the ethnic economy. Even college graduates faced several constraints on occupational choice. According to Stanford University officials, "It is almost impossible to place a Chinese or Japanese of either the first or second generation in any kind of position in engineering, manufacturing, or business" (p. 86). Many firms had regulations barring them from employment. College graduates often ended up working in the ethnic economy, taking positions in landscape gardening and small shops.

Strong bonds of ethnic solidarity, according to Bonacich and Modell, encouraged self-employment as a response to society's rejection. Isolation in self-employment reinforced this solidarity. Japanese employed co-ethnics, offering some protection from the hostility that Japanese employees would have otherwise faced in the general economy. In return, Japanese employers got a loyal, low-wage labor force.

Ethnic solidarity was also manifested in the tanomoshi, or rotating-credit associations, which made loans less costly and easier to acquire than they would have been through commercial banks. These associations represented various sorts of communal ties, and they permitted members to finance small business start-ups and expansion. Solidarity was also implicated in pre-war Japanese business organizations that apparently curtailed internal competition, where possible. Members of these organizations would not impinge upon each other's territories, and they tended not to underprice each other.

After World War II, Japanese in the West were viewed less as hostile aliens and more as abused minorities. As opportunities for employment opened up in the broader economy, employment in the ethnic economy declined quickly. The younger, better educated Japanese were most likely to leave self-employment. "The less education a person received, the more likely he was to be involved in the ethnic economy" (p. 142). The evidence thus suggests that the very high rates of self-employment among the West Coast Japanese were rooted in blocked opportunities. This conclusion is consistent with the fact that the Japanese residing on theEast Coast before World War II, who were less numerous, were not subject to intense racial discrimination, nor did they pursue self-employment at anything approaching the high rates of those on the West Coast.

73. Edna Bonacich and Ivan Light. *Immigrant Entrepreneurs: Koreans in Los Angeles, 1965-1982.* **Berkeley: University of California Press, 1988.**

• According to the 1980 U.S. Census of Population, 22.5 percent of the Koreans in Los Angeles were self-employed or unpaid family workers. Thus, in Los Angeles, Koreans were about three times more frequent in self-employment than non-Koreans.

In 1962, the South Korean government passed an Overseas Immigration Law to encourage emigration as a means of controlling population and alleviating unemployment. Thus, in the 1960s and 1970s, out-migration from Korea rose from a few thousand to tens of thousands a year. Those leaving permanently most often headed for the United States. Economic conditions in Korea made the trip a rational choice for many. During the 1970s, South Korean workers earned about one-tenth the amount of comparable U.S. workers, and they worked an average of 10 extra hours per week (p. 360). A recent history of working long hours at low wages "was a contributory factor to entrepreneurship since it was a necessary ingredient of it" (p. 361).

In one sense, the immigration process further cheapened Korean labor: most came with severe English-language handicaps. This greatly restricted their employment opportunities and pushed many, out of necessity, toward self-employment. Many of the Korean immigrants had professional training in the health professions, but their inability to read and write English frequently made it impossible to take the relevant state of California licensing exams: they were therefore barred from working in their professions.

Koreans often possessed traits that made pursuit of self-employment—in the absence of good alternative employment—a logical decision. Many arrived with college educations, managerial experience, and sufficient savings to finance entry into self-employment. According to Bonacich and Light, many of them were thrifty, ambitious, accustomed to hard work at low pay, and had the ability to use communal and familial resources to develop businesses. They often relied heavily on unpaid family laborers in their firms.

Korean small businesses in Los Angeles have been heavily concentrated in low-income inner city districts that previously had experienced minimal business investment. Korean involvement was common in lines of retailing—gas stations, groceries, liquor stores. Many of the firms operated in predominantly black communities. The question—why did local residents (including minorities) not take advantage of these business opportunities?—has become a popular line of speculation. Bonacich and Light suggested that the long hours and low pay associated with operating such firms is simply unacceptable to most native-born workers. "Most had other job opportunities that paid better, had shorter hours, and provided greater security" (p. 367). But what about the local poor, the unemployed, the welfare recipients, and so forth—why did they not seize the opportunities exploited by the Koreans? The answer, quite simply, is that few of the local poor have the college educations, white-collar work experience, and financial capital resources possessed by so many of the immigrant Korean entrepreneurs.

74. Howard Aldrich, Trevor Jones, and David McEvoy. "Ethnic Advantage and Minority Business Development." In *Ethnic Communities in Business: Strategies for Economic Survival*, edited by Robin Ward and Richard Jenkins. New York: Cambridge University Press, 1984.

• In this study, small retail stores owned by Asians in Great Britain were compared to those owned by whites to identify the cultural and social traits of Asians that may push them toward self-employment. Asian-owned shops differed significantly from those owned by whites in terms of their employment of relatives: an average of 1.4 of the employees of Asian firms were relatives, compared to 0.6 of the employees of white firms. Further, 29 percent of the self-employed Asians employed three or more relatives, particularly extended family members such as mothers and fathers. The greater availability of extended family labor was associated with the greater propensity of Asian retail stores to operate longer each day and to remain open on Sundays.

Relative to whites, a higher proportion of Asians had self-employed fathers. This pattern was accounted for largely by groups of Asian immigrants from East Africa, over three-fourths of whom had self-employed fathers. Many of these Asians from East Africa had been

91

imported to work on British-owned plantations during the colonial era, and others had moved to Great Britain after World War II. Their descendants often pursued self-employment.

The commercial activities of Asian retailers were heavily dependent on ethnic clienteles because, on average, only one-third of their customers were white. This indication of an ethnic enclave economy was confirmed by the high correlation between the proportion of Asian-owned stores and the proportion of Asian residents.

75. Development Associates, Inc. "Attitudes and Inclinations of Minority Youth Toward Business Ownership." An unpublished report to the Minority Business Development Agency of the U.S. Department of Commerce, 1987.

• This study sought to measure the attitudes of minority young adults toward small business ownership. The attitudes and inclinations measured are believed to be associated with the differential business formation rates observed among different racial and ethnic groups and between males and females. A total of 851 young adults (18 to 25 years old) in two metropolitan areas—Washington, D.C., and San Francisco-Oakland, California——were interviewed via telephone, and 538 of them completed and returned supplemental mail-in questionnaires. The four populations of young adults studied were Asians, whites, Hispanics, and blacks.

Six variables were used to measure inclination toward business ownership. One group—blacks—emerged consistently as having the highest inclination toward business ownership. A second clear-cut result was that males—irrespective of race and ethnicity—had greater inclinations toward business ownership than females. The primary variable used to measure ownership inclination was "the respondent's stated probability that he or she would own all or part of a business during his or her lifetime" (p. v).

Asians ranked relatively low on all six variables, showing less inclination toward small business ownership than expected; Asian young adults showed relatively higher inclination toward professional careers. Thus, black young adults show the greatest inclination toward small business ownership, whereas Asian young adults show the greatest inclination toward professional careers (including self-employment in professional practice). The responses among whites and

Hispanics showed mixed patterns across the six indices, with Hispanics ranking slightly lower on self-employment than whites.

A 25-item test was given to rank the attitudes of young adults toward several occupations: doctor, business owner, factory worker, one's current occupation, and one's aspired occupation. The results showed that young adults in all the groups have positive attitudes towards business ownership in terms of leadership, success, and achievement. The disadvantage of having your own business mentioned most often was the limited availability of capital or start-up money. This was a major concern for a higher percentage of blacks than others.

Twenty-seven socio-environmental and parental background variables were analyzed to predict the probability of owning a business. Business ownership by parents emerged as the top predictor for Hispanics, whites, and blacks; for Asians, parental self-employment did not suggest business ownership for young adults. Among blacks, the positive inclination towards business ownership was significantly related to:

- higher socioeconomic status,
- educational attainment expectations,
- greater social integration, and
- parents and relatives as business owner role models.

The high levels of inclination toward small business among black young adults were likely to have been influenced by two survey features. First, black self-employment rates in the two metropolitan areas under consideration are among the highest in the nation. Second, very poor neighborhoods were not included in the sample design. Thus, some caution must be exercised in generalizing the results of this study beyond the limited geographic (and socioeconomic) areas that were considered.

Gaps in Knowledge
Deficiencies in the Existing Body of Literature

Three topics needing research are described below. The first topic—
—entrenched procedures, attitudes, and networks—is very difficult to
investigate, but creative research could crack the problem. Identifying
the discriminatory barriers in the procurement process is an essential
first step. The other two topics—the capacity of minority-owned
business in the absence of discrimination and commercial bank
redlining—could be investigated readily with adequate resources.

Entrenched Procedures, Attitudes, and Networks

Many forms of institutional discrimination defy easy measurement
and are unamenable to the type of quantitative investigation typical of
modern-day social sciences. A combination of innovative research
techniques and old-fashioned anecdotal information is needed to flush
out and identify the many discriminatory practices that handicap
minority-owned businesses. Many of the forms of discrimination tend
to interact with separate but related problems such as bureaucratic
inertia, incompetence, corruption, and sloth, which complicate the
problem of isolating discriminatory practices.

Government Procurement Practices. Even in cases where laws
mandate preferential treatment for minority vendors in the competition
for government procurement dollars, discriminatory barriers are
sometimes rampant. Preferential procurement programs are often
adopted with vague language that does not specify implementation

procedures. Further, adequate staff may be unavailable to implement whatever programs have been placed on the books. Following are some of the problems that arise for potential minority vendors.

• *Certification.* Becoming certified as a minority-owned business ready and willing to accept procurement contracts is often tricky. First, the process of certification is rarely uniform from agency to agency. Minority firms must prepare multiple certification applications, many of which are time-consuming. Sometimes, they must hire professionals to help them complete the relevant forms. Second, the certification forms, once completed, often place the minority firms in limbo, because of the long delays that are common before actual certification. For some government agencies, the number of minorities seeking certification is greater than the number of certified minority-owned businesses. The lengthy procedure diverts minority business resources away from producing and selling products.

• *Bidders' lists.* Certification, if successful, does not guarantee that the minority firms will be notified of relevant procurement opportunities. Sometimes, only firms belonging to entrenched old-boy networks are notified about upcoming procurement opportunities. Often, the firms actually awarded government contracts are not even on the applicable bidders' lists; they simply rely upon established personal relationships with individual government purchasing agents. Minority firms attempting to discover the normal procedures for learning about upcoming procurement opportunities may indeed find that there are no set procedures. Policies may vary from employee to employee within the procurement division. Such unstructured environments put a premium on having close personal relationships with the appropriate government employees—exactly the sort of relationships, of course, that minority firms lacking prior procurement experience are least likely to have. Thus, the status quo often shuts out new minority firms. It is a form of institutionalized discrimination that encourages minority firms to waste time and money getting certified, getting on bidders' lists, and so forth, when, in fact, they have little real opportunity to compete.

• *Contract sizing.* The minority firms attempting to break into government procurement are often small—much smaller than the established nonminority businesses that they are likely to be competing against. The result is that many contracts are too large for them;

they simply do not have the capacity to accept the business. Bidding successfully for an overly large contract has the potential to destroy minority firms, particularly if the government is slow to pay for the goods and services rendered. One way to overcome this obstacle is for procurement officials to downsize many of the contracts. Breaking down very large contracts into smaller components makes them much more accessible to minorities. Some procurement officials feel, however, that downsizing creates too much work for them.

• *Slow payment.* Many government agencies delay payments to vendors for months and months. Many minority firms, often restricted in their access to bank credit, experience liquidity crises (often fatal) due to this slow payment. And since minority firms often work as subcontractors, their general contractors sometimes add another layer of delay by not paying their minority subs promptly after they have been paid by government.

• *Sanctions.* Some government rules and policies that are designed to increase the access of minority businesses to government procurement dollars are routinely violated. Minorities are not notified of available work; they are not paid on time; and prime contractors obtain procurement contracts by agreeing to use minority subs and then do not use them. The sanctions imposed on minority front firms when they are discovered are sometimes trivial or nonexistent. Waivers may be granted to eliminate mandatory minority participation, even when qualified minority firms are ready and willing to participate. The list of violations goes on and on. Quite often these violations of both the letter and the spirit of the law are ignored, and little or no recourse is available to the impacted minority firms. The problem is straightforward: The political will to operate a successful minority business assistance program is simply lacking.

The Construction Industry. Entrenched procedures, discriminatory attitudes, old-boy networks, and the like can undermine minority-owned firms in any line of business, but construction may be in first place when all of the obstacles are tallied. Problems between general contractors and minority subs, discussed above, are certainly rife. Dealing with labor unions in the construction trades adds additional complications that undermine minority business viability. In areas where construction is unionized, the unions act as hiring halls, picking the workers that will be assigned to firms. Union officials often have close working relationships with the established construction firms. A union official may have to decide, for example, whether to allocate his 10 top electricians to a firm owned by his uncle or to a minority business that he is unfamiliar with. The choice may be even more clear-cut: His uncle may shower him with expensive Christmas presents every year. Rightly or wrongly, minority construction firms feel that unions often assign their least productive, least reliable workers to them. Such an allegation is hard to prove, but the example above is typical of the numerous ways in which entrenched old-boy networks help their own.

The construction industry is traditionally one in which general contractors work with a group of closely knit subcontractors. In these old-boy networks, close personal relationships allow subcontractors to maximize their chances of doing business with general contractors. To date, close working relationships between nonminority general contractors and minority subcontractors have been exceedingly rare. And since few minorities are large enough to be general contractors, the old-boy network shuts out minority firms from a fair share of large-scale construction projects.

Bonding and Trade Credit. Other major unexplored areas where restricted access creates severe operating problems for minority-owned firms are bonding and trade credit. Reasons for the restrictions are hard to pin down, since minority firms are frequently smaller and younger relative to their nonminority cohorts. Are they denied bonding because they are young firms and thus have insufficient track records? A vicious circle is suggested: Facing limited access to credit sources such as commercial bank loans, black entrepreneurs form small firms; being small and young, they are denied bonding, which in turn shuts them out of the market for many types of construction work; facing a limited market with limited financial resources, they develop illiquidity problems, which exacerbate their limited access to trade credit. At any point in this vicious circle, nonminority business persons may deny them bonding or credit or whatever, simply because they feel that minorities are generally unreliable. The small, marginal firm forced to operate under such circumstances is likely to remain small and marginal—or it may go broke.

The Capacity of Minority-Owned Business in the Absence of Discrimination

What would the minority business community look like if discrimination did not exist? Barriers to education and training, limited access to financial capital and markets, entrenched old-boy networks, and other factors have discouraged or prevented many minorities from pursuing self-employment. Others have attempted to start their own businesses but have discontinued operations due to some combination of the above constraints. Finally, self-employed minorities often select particular business sectors because they are perceived as the only areas where opportunities exist. These tend to be small lines of business that have low growth prospects, below average profitability, and high failure rates relative to the small business universe.

In the absence of these constraints, what would the minority business community look like? How would the elimination of specific barriers impact the capacity of minority businesses? Precise answers to these questions can probably be obtained from existing data sources. The high level of uncertainty currently surrounding these questions can certainly be reduced substantially.

Studies have identified measurable factors that accurately predict the incidence of self-employment among nonminority males. The likelihood of self-employment among nonminority males is clearly linked to at least four factors: age, sex, education, and net asset holdings. The latter two factors—education and net asset holdings—are the most strongly associated with entering self-employment, and the low incidence of self-employment among minorities is partly explainable in terms of these two factors. In addition, part of the lower incidence of self-employment among minorities—particularly Hispanics—is rooted in their different age distributions. The fraction of the labor force that is self-employed increases with age until the early 40s and then remains constant until the retirement years, when it declines. Minorities are disproportionately more numerous than whites in the younger age brackets. Differences in education and wealth holdings, however, account for most of the lower incidence of self-employment among minorities. College graduates are the group most likely to pursue self-employment in our society. A college degree enhances earning power and, in turn, allows one to accumulate the equity investment that is necessary to launch a business. College education and substantial net

99

asset holdings also enhance borrowing power, another important factor that increases the feasibility of self-employment.

Some barriers to entry vary from industry to industry. In construction, for example, actual work experience in the construction field provides the skills (human capital) needed to make self-employment feasible. Is it harder for the potential minority entrepreneur to parlay this work experience into self-employment? If so, how? Does the minority or female worker require more years of work experience to enter self-employment in construction? Or does their experience have to be matched by larger financial capital investments than the nonminority entrepreneur is required to undertake?

Constance Dunham of the Urban Institute and I are currently investigating the feasibility of answering the "but for discrimination" question. Since set-aside programs set numeric goals for minority business participation, we are pursuing a line of analysis that will directly identify what those numeric goals should be, based on the capacity of the minority business community absent discrimination. For example, if in New Jersey in a given year the actual and potential minority-owned firms have the capacity to be 25 percent of the construction industry in the area , then the state should set a goal of 25 percent that year; that is, it should target 25 percent of the dollar volume of construction spending to minorities for that year. As the capacity of minority firms expands, the percentage should grow accordingly. The capacities of different lines of minority enterprise will undoubtedly vary, and the differences in capacity will be identified and quantified in the course of the study.

A related objective is to link specific barriers responsible for restricting the size and scope of minority business to the capacity of minority businesses to produce. This line of analysis is necessary to effectively link remedial actions contained in set-aside legislation to identified barriers. Specifying appropriate remedies is essential for a program seeking to alleviate discriminatory barriers and thus to close the gap between present-day underdevelopment and minority business potential, absent discrimination.

Redlining, Capital Gaps, and Minority Business Viability

The Supreme Court's references in *Richmond* v. *Croson* to "statistical proof" of discrimination indicate that detailed data on business characteristics are required if state and local government minority business set-asides are to survive. The evidence in the Characteristics of Business Owners (CBO) data base of differential treatment of black-owned firms by commercial banks typifies appropriate statistical proof: a set-aside program that assisted firms handicapped by such treatment (as described in "Capital Issues and Minority-Owned Business" [no. 52] and in "Small Business Viability in the Urban Ghetto" [no. 54]) would be able to cite the "passive participant" doctrine to justify its actions.

This discussion is designed to illustrate that the CBO data base can be applied to both the design and implementation of programs that seek to remedy racial discrimination and the litigation on minority business issues. Findings to date strongly support the hypothesis that commercial bank redlining undermines the viability of black businesses operating in minority communities. Additional investigation is needed to guide public policy and, if appropriate, to influence the outcome of litigation involving minority business programs.

The hypothesis which needs to be investigated is that minority communities experience a capital gap due, in part, to the smaller loans available to business startups receiving commercial bank financing. Banks are, in fact, the largest single source of debt used by minorities entering business. A capital gap is determined to exist if (controlling for the owner's age, education, managerial experience, equity investment in the small business, and so forth) the locational variable—the firm's location—is inversely related to bank loan amount and the relationship is statistically significant. This hypothesis would have to be investigated from several angles.

• *Do banks give minority firms smaller loan amounts because the firms are located in minority neighborhoods or because of the race or ethnicity of the owner?* Variables measuring race of owner and business location have been found to be highly correlated. Findings to date consistently suggest that the locational variable is the cause of smaller loan amounts, not the race of the owner. This is why the label "redlining" is appropriate: It appears that banks are applying discriminatory treatment to the minority community rather than to business owners. But the number of minority firms operating in nonminority areas is small. Thus, this issue needs to be re-investigated with much larger samples of bank loan recipients before we can

101

conclusively rule out loan discrimination based solely on owner race. Finally, the finding that bank discrimination applies solely to certain geographic areas implies that remedies should be focused on the impacted areas—the minority communities—rather than on all minority business owners.

• *Do banks discriminate against white small firms located in minority neighborhoods?* The evidence to date suggests weakly that they do, but the number of white firms operating in minority communities severely reduces the applicable sample size. Larger sample sizes from the 1987 CBO database are needed to resolve this issue.

• *Do banks redline small firms in minority areas because the communities are composed of minorities or because the communities are poor?* Variables measuring community economic well-being and racial composition have been found to be very highly correlated. Further, it is quite possible that high minority composition and poverty are additive, suggesting that poor minority areas are more heavily redlined than affluent minority areas. The relative impacts of community racial composition and economic well-being on bank lending behavior clearly need to be disentangled.

The evidence to date indicates that race is much more important than poverty (or lack thereof) in explaining redlining. However, small sample size once again reduces the reliability of the conclusion. Specifically, a larger sample of firms is needed to achieve an adequate representation of businesses in affluent black communities.

• *Do banks have different lending practices for different minority communities?* Existing evidence indicates that black areas are hit harder by redlining than Hispanic neighborhoods, but this has not been tested rigorously.

• *Neighborhood minority composition notwithstanding, are banks more likely to redline declining neighborhoods than improving communities?* And how should "declining" and "improving" be measured? Does a bank view a low-income minority community as improving if high-income whites are moving in? It would be a straightforward matter to investigate the declining community hypothesis by controlling simultaneously for several relevant factors—minority composition, economic well-being, and overall population within the applicable geographic area.

Finally, all of the above questions need to be investigated at the state and local levels. This is possible, at present, for large areas such as Los Angeles and the state of Pennsylvania.

Existing findings (see "Small Business Viability in the Urban Ghetto"; no. 54) indicate that commercial bank redlining is a major obstacle to the development of black business in urban minority communities. Controlling for owner age, years of education, equity capital investment, and other factors, banks were found to lend nearly $40,000 less, on average, to black firms located in minority neighborhoods than to black firms in nonminority areas. The primary consideration in determining bank loan amount for black business start-ups is the geographic location of the firm: Owner educational background and equity investment are less important than location.

Commercial banks redline minority communities in general—not just the core regions of the poverty ghetto that have intense poverty and racial segregation. Black firms located in minority communities are very small, in part, because their access to credit is restricted: their loan applications are less likely to be approved, and when they are, the loan amounts are substantially less than those received by their cohorts in nonminority areas.

The statistical documentation of redlining described above identifies a specific type of race-based treatment that tends to undermine the viability of black firms. Such statistical descriptions of discrimination have acquired an enormous new relevancy in the wake of the January 1989 Supreme Court ruling (*Richmond* v. *Croson*) that Richmond, Virginia's minority business set-aside program "violates the dictates of the Equal Protection Clause." In the post-*Croson* era, government programs that attempt to remedy racial discrimination are apt to be subject to judicial challenge unless the discrimination is precisely and thoroughly documented. Justice Sandra Day O'Connor wrote in the *Croson* ruling that "Nothing we say today precludes a state or local entity from taking action to rectify the effects of identified discrimination within the jurisdiction." Furthermore, she stated, "evidence of a pattern of individual discriminatory acts can, if supported by *appropriate statistical proof,* lend support to a local government's determination that broader remedial relief is justified." Finally, O'Connor stated that "Any public entity, state or federal, has a compelling interest in assuring that public dollars. . . do not serve to finance the evil of private

103

prejudice. . . . if the city could show that it had essentially become a 'passive participant' in a system of racial exclusion . . . the city could take affirmative steps to dismantle such a system."

Historical Overview
The Black Business Community
Before World War II

A long-term perspective on the factors that have shaped black business is needed to understand today's dual trends of decline and growth in the traditional and emerging sectors of black business enterprise. The traditional black business was shaped by a specific time period—the 19th century—and a specific region—the South. Black entrepreneurship was originally an offspring of the pre-Civil War South, where certain lowly lines of business were believed to be "appropriate" for former slaves.

Before the Civil War. Prior to the Civil War, free blacks were prominent in lines of business that used the skills and personality traits they had acquired as slaves. Since white entrepreneurs tended to avoid businesses of servile status, blacks in many communities had little competition in select fields. Their success in barbershop and beauty parlor operations, cooking and catering, cleaning and pressing, and shoe shine and repair has been seen as shrewd capitalization of social proscription (Harris 1936). An affluent white clientele—naturally inclined to be served by the Negro—provided the patronage for many of the successful black-owned firms during the 19th century.

In no trade was the reputation of blacks more secure than in cooking. Black caterer Peter Augustin, for example, who entered business in Philadelphia in 1818, had a reputation for courtesy and efficiency that spread throughout the eastern United States (Du Bois 1899). Augustin and his successors had the loyal patronage of Philadelphia's high society for most of the 19th century. Throughout the South and the urban Northeast, blacks ran popular eating establishments that relied on affluent white patrons.

Businesses requiring accounting skills and considerable capital were naturally the least common lines of enterprise operated by free blacks. Even if the technical and economic obstacles could be overcome, the hostility of the white community would destroy black firms that they thought were socially inappropriate. By the mid-19th century, most southern states had passed laws forbidding blacks from engaging in any line of business that required the ability to read and write. In the North, blacks were denied the right to sue, and black merchants were generally unable to obtain trade credit. Blacks endured only in those fields that were consistent with the subservient status of the freed slave (Bates 1973a).

Regional diversity in the business activities of black entrepreneurs reflected a complex array of social attitudes and institutional racial constraints. In Louisiana, freed blacks participated in a wide array of business activities. A pattern of race relations reflecting Caribbean influences persisted in that state until well beyond 1803. "The Haitian migration of skilled and educated Creoles in the mid-1790s and again in the early 1800s, before the American purchase, assured the entrenchment of free men of color in both skilled and white collar occupations" (Walker 1986). White family connections sometimes contributed to the success of black-owned firms in Louisiana. In her study of 21 wealthy (net worth exceeding $100,000) antebellum black entrepreneurs, Walker noted that "only four accumulated their wealth outside the state of Louisiana" (p. 352).

The large and successful black business community in New Orleans prospered as long as social attitudes were tolerant. But an increasingly hostile racial climate in the 1850s led to a decline in black business participation. A handbook of wealthy citizens of Philadelphia (property holdings exceeding $50,000 was the wealth criterion) published in 1846 listed four self-employed blacks. Their lines of business— hairdresser, sailmaker, farmer, and lumber merchant—reflected the diversity of the black business community in the Philadelphia region. The regional patterns of black business development in the antebellum period were a reflection of societal constraints of varying intensity.

The story of the skilled black artisan from prior to the Civil War to the post-Reconstruction era illustrates how profoundly discrimination has undermined and distorted black entrepreneurship. Blacks at one time dominated many skilled trades in the South. Rather than depend on white labor, slavemasters typically trained their own slaves in carpentry, blacksmithing, and other skilled trades. Slave mechanics were often allowed to hire out on their own in return for a fixed sum of money or a percentage of their earnings. Skilled white workers appealed to government, demanding that blacks be legally restricted to menial jobs. Their efforts were largely unsuccessful, however, because planter-dominated legislatures saw limitations on slave labor as a threat to the value of their property. At the end of the Civil War, an estimated 100,000 of a total 120,000 artisans in the southern states were black (Kelsey 1903).

Effects of Emancipation. However, emancipation and the post-Reconstruction era unfairly handicapped the black artisan class. No longer protected by the slave-owners, black artisans had to compete in a free, unprotected market, whereas whites were often protected by craft unions and Jim Crow institutions. South Carolina, for example, required after 1865 that blacks purchase licenses for a fee of $10 annually before working as artisans, mechanics, and shopkeepers. Whites were not required to pay license fees (Ransom and Sutch 1977). Craft unionism, with its apprenticeship system, was particularly effective in diminishing the ranks of black artisans in the North. Excluding blacks from craft unions was more typical in the heavily unionized northern cities than in the South (Bates and Fusfeld 1984).

The abolition of slavery brought about a decline in the number of black-owned businesses for several reasons. The post-war South was in the grips of a severe depression, and it offered few opportunities for accumulating the capital necessary to establish businesses. The blacks who established firms in retail fields were additionally handicapped by the economic structure of the rural South. Most blacks were then living in the rural South and they relied on their landlord or the company store (see Pierce 1947) for their retail needs. If landlords did not run their own commissaries, they made arrangements with local white merchants to supply their tenant farmers' needs. This system effectively isolated black merchants from most of their potential clientele.

The strongholds of black business in the late 19th century differed little from the strongholds of black business before the Civil War. In addition to failing to establish themselves in new lines of business, black entrepreneurs were undercut in their traditional fields by late 19th century immigrants. These immigrants were willing to compete with blacks in personal services industries, and they were quick to exploit business opportunities in embryonic urban black communities. The number of black-owned businesses did not increase substantially until World War I.

The early black businesses, founded most commonly to serve whites, gradually lost their white patronage after emancipation. "The Negro caterer has slowly been losing ground, probably through loss of personal contact with the fashionable group whose first thought used to be for the Negro when service of any kind was to be done" (Fleming and Sheldon 1938, 114). Those with experience in food preparation and personal services survived by increasing their black patrons. However, black retailers had never experienced appreciable white patronage. Whites could open stores in black areas, but black merchants were usually kept out of white neighborhoods. The white businessman operating in the ghetto, able to command more capital and credit than the typical black entrepreneur, has always had a competitive edge.

The 20th Century. During World War I, industrial jobs were abundant in the urban black communities. The wave of 1919 race riots in Chicago, Washington, and many other cities aroused urban blacks to a high state of racial consciousness. Blacks in urban centers came together for mutual help and protection and quickly grasped the notion of building and supporting their own business enterprises. The financial constraints that had restricted black entrepreneurs for so long were eased for many of them during the prosperous war years. A "buy black" sentiment prevailed, and many black businesses were financed by churches and fraternal lodges, whose members would become loyal patrons of the newly formed firms. A conspicuous example of the increasing racial consciousness was the development of black newspapers. A black-owned printing industry arose as black publications multiplied.

In the 1920s, black businesses were increasingly commonplace in all areas of the United States. An estimated 70,000 black establishments were operating by 1930, a 700 percent increase over 1900. Progress was particularly evident in the life insurance industry, where in 1928, 32 firms employed over 6,000 agents and controlled over $18 million in assets (Harmon, Lindsay, and Woodson 1929, 7-8). These were the

108

golden years for the urban black business community.

The Great Depression destroyed many of the gains of the previous decade. Black retailers, who had often relied on the loyalty of black consumers to remain viable, lost their clients in droves. Black merchants cried that they were being abandoned by their race; black consumers responded that they were being exploited by the racial appeals of black merchants. "What the Negro businessman wants is to monopolize and exploit the market the black population provides" (Harris 1936, 184).

Access to financial capital and trade credit was limited, further constraining the development of black enterprise. White ghetto merchants have always enjoyed greater access to credit than black merchants, and this advantage often proved to be decisive during the depressed 1930s. In 1944, Gunnar Myrdal observed that:

> The Negro businessman encounters greater difficulties than whites in securing credit. This is partially due to the marginal position of Negro business. It is also partly due to prejudicial opinions among whites concerning business ability and personal reliability of Negroes. In either case a vicious circle is in operation keeping Negro business down. (Myrdal 1944, 308)

Thus, we see that discrimination has played many roles in shaping black business enterprise. Discrimination in the labor market made it difficult for blacks to accumulate the initial equity investment that is required to create firms. The lack of black-owned construction companies in unionized urban areas was caused partially by the traditional practice of barring blacks from entering apprentice programs in the building trades. In addition, limited educational opportunities have always handicapped the black business community. The blacks who were lured into the world of business in the 1920s were typically not the ones who were highly educated. Between 1912 and 1938, for example, 73 percent of black college graduates became preachers or teachers (Holsey 1938, 241-2). Those who attended college were restricted by social attitudes about which occupations were appropriate for blacks. Medicine, dentistry, and law were open to a fortunate few, but black college graduates were rarely found in fields such as engineering, accounting, and general business.

These and other constraints produced a black business community that consisted largely of very small frms concentrated in a few lines of business—beauty parlors, barbershops, restaurants, dry cleaners, shoe shiners, and mom and pop food stores.

Data Bases Used in the Studies

In this appendix, the data bases that were used in three or more of the studies reviewed in this bibliography are described.

Survey of Minority-Owned Business Enterprises (SMOBE)

The SMOBE data files were used by more of the authors in this bibliography than any other single data source. The SMOBE data have been compiled at five-year intervals in recent years: the most recent data available are for 1987.

General description. The U.S. Bureau of the Census compiles the SMOBE data for three groups: blacks, Hispanics, and other minorities. The SMOBE compiles data on firm characteristics from two sources: income tax return tabulations and survey data. The SMOBE data are made public in aggregate forms; the firms are grouped by geographic location, industry, and employer status. Thus, for example, one can use the SMOBE data to calculate mean sales in 1982 for black-owned construction firms in Baltimore that used paid employees. In general, the SMOBE does not provide detailed data on firms unless the number in the area under consideration is quite large. In Minneapolis, for example, The SMOBE indicates that in 1982, there were 554 black-owned firms. Yet, it provides no information on mean sales by industry for industries such as manufacturing (12 firms) and wholesale (5 firms), because the number of black-owned firms in Minneapolis was too low to reveal this without violating prevailing standards on data confidentiality and disclosure. In geographic areas with fewer than 1,000 minority-owned firms, the SMOBE provides very little detailed information on industry-specific groups of firms.

Strong points. Since the SMOBE data are published at five-year intervals, it is possible to calculate changes in the composition of minority business over time, by industry group as well as by region (in regions with numerous minority firms). At substantial cost, it is possible to request special tabulations of the SMOBE data from the Census Bureau.

Weak points. The data on blacks are more accurate than the data on Hispanics and other minorities. The social security records used to identify blacks are less well suited to identify other minorities such as Hispanics; prior to 1981, racial group data were limited to whites, blacks, others. The SMOBE conducts minority business surveys to try to rectify this problem. However, the data on specific regions are particularly suspect when they describe minority groups other than blacks. In addition, the SMOBE is constantly changing its methodology in ways that introduce multiple inconsistencies when one compares different years. Recent changes in the method made minority firms more numerous in 1982 than they would have been using 1977 data. For example, in 1977, two firms owned by the same person would have been counted as one combined firm by the SMOBE; in 1982, they would have been counted as two separate firms. Finally, the SMOBE includes everyone who files a schedule C income tax return as a business owner, even those who are full-time employees and report very small amounts of self-employment income. In 1982, for example, over 30 percent of all of the minority-owned "businesses" covered by the SMOBE were schedule C tax return filers who had total receipts from self-employment of under $5,000. Thus, the SMOBE tends to overstate the number of minority-owned firms and to understate the average annual sales per firm.

Citations. Studies described in this bibliography that used data from the SMOBE include:

- Bates 1983 (no. 13) and 1984 (no. 61).
- Markwalder 1981 (no. 12)
- Simms and Burbridge 1986 (no. 58)
- Stevens 1984 (no. 31)

- Suggs 1986 (no. 28)
- Swinton and Handy 1983 (no. 39) and 1984 (no. 59)
- Woolf 1986 (no. 57)

Small Business Administration (SBA) Data

The SMOBE provides the smallest amount of detail on minority-owned firms of any of the data bases, but it is the most accessible. It is difficult to gain access to the SBA data on minority firms, since each request to use the data must pass through a slow review process, which may or may not lead to approval. In its computer, the SBA has files describing many tens of thousands of firms that have gotten either bank loans guaranteed by the SBA or direct loans from the SBA.

General description. For all loans that have been approved, the SBA maintains records of the firm's business characteristics, loan terms, loan repayment status, and the owner's demographic traits such as race and sex. At its regional offices, the SBA maintains more detailed data on each of the loans approved, including income statements and balance sheets (both business and personal).

Strong points. Since detailed data are available for individual businesses, it is possible to set up all sorts of different business groups and subsets. Common groupings are race, ethnicity, sex of owner, industry group, presence or absence of paid employees, and loan repayment status. In contrast to the SMOBE, the records in the SBA data base really are small businesses, as opposed to employees reporting small amounts of self-employment income.

Weak points. The SBA data do not represent the universe of small business. They represent only the universe of those whose loan applications were approved under SBA programs. Finally, the data are hard to access, as explained above.

Citations. Studies described in this bibliography that relied on SBA data include:

- Bates 1973c (no. 7); 1973a (no. 9); 1973b (no. 10); 1975 (no. 14); 1974 (no.15); 1983b (no. 18)
- Bates and Bradford 1979 (no. 20)
- Bates and Hester 1977 (no. 53b)
- Johnson 1980 (no. 19)
- Klein 1978 (no. 17)

Public Use Sample (PUS)

The Census Bureau compiles population data for the Public Use Sample (PUS) at 10-year intervals: the most recent data are for 1980. The 1980 PUS consists of 5 percent of the household records covered in the decennial census, available on computer tape. In a sense, these data are easily accessible, but the 1980 PUS is so large that it is unwieldy: It takes up over 100 standard (1,600 BPI) large magnetic tapes. Reading through all of the tapes can easily cost thousands of dollars.

General description. The PUS provides detailed data on individual self-employed persons, including extensive demographic data, educational background, occupation, income by source, geographic location of the home and work place, and so forth.

Strong points. In contrast to the SMOBE, persons are identified according to their primary labor force attachment, which means that it is possible to sort recipients into groups having self-employment (as opposed to wage and salary work) as their primary activity in the labor market. The PUS sample is large enough to permit area-specific analyses of minority firms in states where minorities are numerous and in individual large cities and SMSAs. Because the PUS consist of data on individual self-employed persons, it is easy for the researcher to establish numerous business subsets to highlight such features as industry group, geographic area, and various owner demographic traits. Because the data are available at 10-year intervals, one can trace the changing composition of minority business through time. The 1970 PUS, however, provides less geographic detail about the location of individuals; 1970-1980 PUS comparisons are easiest to conduct at the statewide level.

Weak points. The PUS focuses on the traits of self-employed persons but it contains nothing directly about the traits of the businesses themselves, such as annual sales, employees, financial capital investment, and so forth. In addition, the PUS has treated Hispanics inconsistently over the years; one must be very careful when comparing Hispanic self-employed groups in 1970 and 1980.

Citations. Studies that used PUS data. The studies in this bibliography that used data from the PUS are:
- Bates 1987 (no. 26); 1986 (no. 41); 1988a (no. 44)
- Fratoe and Meeks 1988 (no. 27)

Dun's Financial Profiles (DFP)

The DFP originates from Dun and Bradstreet's (D and B) credit reporting activities. Dun and Bradstreet requests income statements and balance sheets from the five million plus small firms in its master file. Those that respond and whose balance sheets and income statements meet the quality control standards are included in the DFP. Thus, the DFP contains extensive balance sheet and income statement data on approximately 800,000 firms. Unfortunately, minority status cannot be identified for the DFP records. The Minority Business Development Agency of the U.S. Department of Commerce undertook a widespread compilation of the names and addresses of minority firms. They were drawn from minority business directories maintained largely by corporations and government agencies seeking to direct procurement dollars toward minority firms. The directories yielded a list of over 20,000 businesses, which were matched against the DFP. Over 3,000 matches were obtained, yet 51 percent of the matches had to be dropped because a substantial portion of the information in the DFP was inadequate. In other words, the firm-specific DFP data are haphazard. The outcome of this whole process was a data file of nearly 1,500 minority-owned firms for which comprehensive balance sheet and income statement data are available on a firm-by-firm basis.

General description. First, the DFP data on minority businesses do not represent a random selection of minority firms. Firms in the data base found their way into D and B files because other businesses inquired about their creditworthiness. Second, firms were included in the DFP only if they had prepared rather extensive and internally consistent balance sheets and income statements. Third, a firm's presence in a minority business directory most commonly meant that it was the sort with the potential to sell to large corporations or government agencies. Finally, the data for each firm in the final data file are extensive; they include employment, industry, sales, profits, balance sheet information, and so forth. A more detailed description of this data base appears in Bates and Furino, 1985.

Strong points. The minority businesses in the DFP are larger and more successful than those in the universe of small firms. They are disproportionately concentrated in nontraditional lines of minority business such as manufacturing, wholesale, business services, and large scale construction. If one wants to focus on the types of firms that are likely to participate in minority business procurement and set-

115

aside programs, then the DFP data are appropriate. Finally, a matching sample of nonminority businesses was selected from the DFP files; it is therefore possible to conduct minority-nonminority comparative analyses.

Weak points. The DFP provides very little information about the traits of minority business owners, such as demographic characteristics, educational background, and so forth.

Citations. The studies in this bibliography that used data from the DFP are:

- Bates 1985c (no. 24a); 1985b (no. 24b); and 1985a (no. 40)
- DETAS 1983 (no. 50).

The Characteristics of Business Owners (CBO) Data Base

General description. The U.S. Bureau of the Census compiled the CBO data base in 1987 using a questionnaire. The data base consists of five panels, each containing data on 25,000 persons who were self-employed in 1982. The five panels are as follows: Panel One, Hispanic; Panel Two, other minority (largely Asian); Panel Three, black; Panel Four, female (minority as well as nonminority); Panel Five, white male.

Data are included on several variables that measure qualitative and quantitative aspects of human capital.

- The highest year of schooling completed is measured at three levels: (1) elementary, (2) high school, and (3) college.
- The presence or absence of formal business schooling is measured by attendance in business education courses or seminars.
- Labor force experience is measured quantitatively two ways: (1) number of years of employment experience before entering business and (2) number of those years employed spent in a managerial capacity.
- Previous exposure to small business is captured by questions on (1) small business exposure within one's family and (2) whether any other business was owned prior to the one owned in 1982.
- Labor input quantity is gauged by counting the average number of hours per week spent managing or working in one's small business during 1982.

In addition to providing an extensive profile of owner human capital characteristics, the CBO data base contains four variables that describe the labor force of the firms that use paid employees: (1) number of employees during the pay period including March 12, 1982, (2) total 1982 payroll, (3) percentage of employees that were women, and (4) percentage of employees that were minorities.

Other variables that describe the business owners include marital status, age, sex, and ethnicity. The race and ethnicity codes focus largely on breakdowns of the Hispanic and other minority samples: Chinese, Japanese, Asian Indian, Korean, Filipino, Hawaiian, Vietnamese, American Indian, Mexican, Cuban, Puerto Rican, and European Spanish, among others. Other owner traits included in the CBO data base include year of entry into self-employment and percentage of total income derived from self-employment.

The record of each business owner also includes an extensive list of business characteristics such as the firm's four-digit SIC code and its legal form of organization (proprietorship, partnership, or corporation). Also included are the firm's 1982 annual sales and its profits before taxes. Data on the owner's investment in the small business include the dollar value of total financial capital inputs, the percentage of financial capital that was borrowed, and the sources that provided debt capital: commercial banks, family, friends, former owners, and so forth. Geographic variables include the state, county, SMSA, and zip code of the business location.

Although the CBO data base consists entirely of small firms that were operating in 1982, the questionnaire was not mailed out until late 1986. A powerful question—"Is the business you owned in 1982 still operating?"—was therefore added in an attempt to quantify small business failure rates. This information opened up the possibility of investigating relationships between firm survival and owner human capital, as well as other owner and firm traits.

The unit of observation, or the record, in the CBO data base is the owner, but straightforward transformations make it possible to focus on the firms. Each record has an owner weight and a firm weight to make the panel represent the relevant universe, and the appropriate weight must be used when examining groups of panels. Minority-owned firms, for example, can be examined by combining panels one through three and applying the firm weights.

Strong points. This survey of 125,000 self-employed individuals is unlike any other large-scale small business survey that has been undertaken to date. Other sources, such as the PUS, which uses samples from the decennial population census, describe self-employed people as individuals; periodic business census data (1982, 1977. . .) describe businesses. The CBO survey is the first very large data base that describes self-employed people as individuals as well as the traits of the firms these people own: sales, employees, annual payroll, earnings, financial capital input, and so forth.

The sampling universe consisted of persons who filed one of the following income tax returns in 1982: Schedule C, Form 1040 (sole proprietorships); Form 1065 (owners of partnerships); and Form 1120S (owners of Subchapter S business corporations). Census questionnaires covering both owner and business traits were sent out to 125,000 persons, and over 81 percent of them were returned. The CBO data base is, therefore, broadly similar to the SMOBE data base. Unlike the SMOBE, however, the CBO contains large samples of nonminority self-employed persons, which allows direct comparisons of minority and nonminority populations. CBO data on minority and nonminority businesses in 1987 are scheduled for release in 1991.

Weak points. One problem inherent in the design of the CBO data base stems from the fact that self-employment and small business ownership are not synonymous. The question "How did you acquire ownership of this business?" is likely to be confusing to a person who hosted a Tupperware party five years ago. Self-employment activities are supplemental for many people whose main labor force status is "employee." Many are operating "casual" businesses, particularly those who file schedule C income tax forms. Quite frequently, these casual business owners have invested no financial capital into their "firms," and their revenues from self-employment are quite low. Over half of the 1982 records show sales of under $10,000. Low sales amounts are most pronounced in the female business panel, where 49.7 percent of the overall sample reported 1982 sales of less than $5,000. One technique for deleting these casual businesses is to define small business firms as the subset of the CBO sample for which financial capital investment in the business was greater than zero and annual sales in 1982 were at least $5,000. Applying these restrictions reduces the number of records in each panel by at least 50 percent. Finally, the CBO is ideally suited for analyzing specific states and large

SMSAs where minority residents are numerous. The sample sizes are too small, however, to analyze many of the SMSAs such as Richmond, Virginia, that might benefit from access to a data base as comprehensive as the CBO.

The CBO data base, despite its comprehensiveness, suffers from some of the typical drawbacks of relatively new data bases, as well as a few unique complications. Available documentation is incomplete, sometimes confusing, and generally inadequate. To use the CBO data, a researcher should ideally plan to spend at least a month getting familiar with the data base. Gaining access to the actual data, however, is not easy. It requires gaining the appropriate government security clearances, paying $200 per day to use Census Bureau facilities, and working at the Suitland, Maryland, headquarters building of the Census Bureau. In light of the tremendous potential value of the CBO data for cities and states seeking to justify programs to assist minority enterprise, the inaccessibility is tragic.

Citations. The studies in this bibliography that used CBO data are:

- Bates 1988b (no. 65); 1989a (no. 71); 1989b (no. 36); 1989c (no. 54); 1992 (nos. 29, 51, 60, 64, 66, and 68)
- Bates and Nucci 1989 (no. 34b)
- Fratoe 1988 (no. 32)

Glossary of Technical Terms

Capital-labor ratio: "Capital" in this context refers to the plant and equipment used by businesses to produce goods and services. A low capital-labor ratio indicates that business is producing goods and/or services in a labor intensive fashion, that is, large quantities of labor are used relative to plant and equipment. A high capital-labor ratio indicates that the production process of the business is capital intensive, that is, it uses very little labor relative to plant and equipment. Note that modern oil refineries are capital intensive; garment factories, in contrast, are labor intensive.

Discriminant analysis: This is a statistical technique used to distinguish between two groups—active versus discontinued businesses, for example—by selecting discriminating variables measuring the traits on which the groups are expected to differ. Mathematically, the objective of discriminant analysis is to weigh and combine the variables in a fashion that forces the groups to be as statistically distinct as possible. One seeks to discriminate between the groups in the sense of being able to tell them apart.

Economies of scale: This term is more properly expressed as "economies of large-scale production." Economies of scale are present when businesses have low production costs per unit of output as a result of large production facilities. Economies of scale are typical in modern oil refineries; garment factories typically lack economies of scale.

Multiple regression analysis (also referred to as regression model or regression equation): This statistical technique allows the simultaneous effects of many factors to be taken into account in determining some phenomenon. For example, the phenomenon to be determined may the level of business sales in 1982, which is thought to have been influenced by five separate factors: owner age, sex, education, amount of time spent working in the business, and level of financial investment in the firm. Multiple regression analysis examines these five factors that may explain business sales levels and determines which are important determinants of sales. It also identifies the relative importance of each of the five factors in explaining sales. Multiple regression analysis is the statistical tool used most widely by social scientists.

Multiplier effects: The multiplier is the factor that relates any change in spending on goods and services to the resulting change in the dollar value of goods and services produced. Thus, a multiplier of two for a region indicates that a one million dollar increase in spending will cause an ultimate two million dollar increase in the output of goods and services for the region.

Opportunity costs: These are the benefits or satisfactions that could have been obtained by choosing something else. For the person who works full-time running a small business, the opportunity costs are the benefits that could have been obtained by choosing, instead, to work as an employee.

Vertical integration: Vertical integration has to do with the number of steps in a manufacturing process that a firm performs. If a firm performs one or two steps in a 10-step manufacturing process, it has low vertical integration; if the firm performs nine or 10 of the steps, it has high vertical integration. IBM, for example, has high vertical integration.

Author Index
& Works Cited

In the righthand column, boldfaced page numbers indicate the pages where titles are fully reviewed. The non-bold page numbers indicate places where the title is mentioned in the course of another review. Note that some titles are reviewed more than once in this volume for separate treatments of chapters or topics. —— ed.

Aldrich, Howard, Trever Jones, and David McEvoy. 1984. "Ethnic Advantage and Minority Business Development." In Robin Ward and Richard Jenkins, eds., *Ethnic Communities in Business: Strategies for Economic Survival.* New York: Cambridge University Press.   **91**

American Council on Education. 1988. *Seventh Annual Status Report.* Washington, D.C.   **51**

Ando, Faith. 1988. "Capital Issues and Minority-Owned Business," *The Review of Black Political Economy*, Vol. 16 (Spring, 1988), pp. 77-109.   56, **63**, 79, 101

Bates, Timothy. 1973a. *Black Capitalism: A Quantitative Analysis.* New York: Praeger.   6, **13**, 106, 113

_____. 1973b. "An Econometric Analysis of Lending to Black Businessmen." *The Review of Economics and Statistics*, Vol. 55 (August 1973), pp. 272-83.   6, **15**, 20, 113

_____. 1973c. "The Potential of Black Capitalism." *Public Policy*, Vol. 21 (Winter 1973), pp. 135-48.   6, **11**, 113

_____. 1974. "Financing Black Enterprises." *The Journal of Finance*, Vol. 29 (June 1974), pp. 747-61.   19, **20**, 62, 113

_____. 1975. "Government as Financial Intermediary for Minority Entrepreneurs." *The Journal of Business*, Vol. 48 (October 1975), pp. 541-57.   15, **19**, 23, 113

_____. 1978. "Capital Markets and the Potential of Black Entrepreneurship." *Public Policy*, Vol. 26 (Summer 1978), pp. 477-9.   27

_____. 1981. "Black Entrepreneurship and Government Programs," *Journal of Contemporary Studies*, Vol. 4 (Fall 1981), pp. 59-70.   **31**

_____. 1982. "A Review of the Small Business Administra-tion's Major Loan Programs." In *Studies of Small Business Finance—A Report to Congress*, by the Interagency Task Force on Small Business. Washington, D.C.   24

_____. 1983a. "The Potential for Black Business: A Comment." *The Review of Black Political Economy*, Vol. 12 (Winter 1983), pp. 237-40.   **17**, 112

_____. 1983b. "Small Business Administration Loan Programs." In Paul Horvitz and R. Richardson Pettit, eds., *Sources of Financing for Small Business*. Greenwich, Conn.: JAI Press, 1983.   **23**, 113

_____. 1984-85. "Urban Economic Transformation and Minority Business Opportunities." *The Review of Black Political Economy,* Vol. 13 (Winter 1984-85), pp. 21-36.

74, 112

_____. 1985a. "Entrepreneur Human Capital and Minority Business Viability." *The Journal of Human Resources,* Vol. 20 (Fall 1985), pp. 540-54.

49, 116

_____. 1985b. "Impact of Preferential Procurement Policies on Minority-Owned Businesses." *The Review of Black Political Economy,* Vol. 14 (Summer 1985), pp. 51-66.

29, 116

_____. 1985c. "Minority Business Set-Asides: Theory and Practice." In U.S. Commission on Civil Rights, *Affirmative Action in Employment and Minority Business Set-Asides.* Washington, D.C.: Government Printing Office.

29, 116

_____. 1986. "Characteristics of Minorities Who Are Entering Self-Employment." *The Review of Black Political Economy,* Vol. 15 (Fall 1986), pp.31-49.

50, 114

_____. 1987. "Self-Employed Minorities: Traits and Trends." *Social Science Quarterly,* Vol. 68 (September 1987), pp. 539-51.

34, 114

_____. 1988a. *An Analysis of Income Differentials Among Self-Employed Minorities.* Los Angeles: UCLA Center for Afro-American Studies.

53, 114

_____. 1988b. "Do Black-Owned Businesses Employ Minority Workers? New Evidence." *The Review of Black Political Economy,* Vol. 16 (Spring 1988), pp. 51-64.

72, **79**, 112

_____. 1989a. "The Changing Nature of Minority Business: A Comparative Analysis of Asian, Nonminority, and Black-Owned Businesses." *The Review of Black Political Economy*, Vol. 18 (Fall 1989), pp. 25-42.   15, **87**, 119

_____. 1989b. "Entrepreneur Factor Inputs and Small Business Longevity." Discussion paper, U.S. Bureau of the Census, Center for Economic Studies (June 1989). Washington, D.C.   44, **46**, 119

_____. 1989c. "Small Business Viability in the Urban Ghetto." *Journal of Regional Science*, Vol. 29 (November 1989), pp. 625-43.   56, 63, **65**, 79, 101, 103, 119

_____. 1990. "Entrepreneur Human Capital Inputs and Small Business Longevity." *The Review of Economics and Statistics*, Vol. 72 (November 1990), pp. 551-59.   44, **47**

_____. 1992 (forthcoming). *Banking on Black Enterprise: The Potential of Emerging Firms for Revitalizing Urban Economies.* Washington, D.C.: Joint Center for Political and Economic Studies.   34, **39**, **54**, 56, **61**, 71, **72**, **77**, **80**, **82**, 119

_____, and William Bradford. 1979. *Financing Black Economic Development.* New York: Academic Press.   4, 19, **25**, 113

_____, and Antonio Furino. 1985. "A New Nationwide Data Base for Minority Business." *Journal of Small Business Management*, Vol. 23 (April 1985), pp. 41-52.   115

_____, and Daniel Fusfeld. 1984. *The Political Economy of the Urban Ghetto.* Carbondale, IL.: Southern Illinois University Press.   72, **74**, 107

_____, and Donald Hester. 1977. "Analysis of a Commercial Bank Minority Lending Program: Comment." *Journal of Finance*, Vol. 32 (December 1977), pp. 1783-9.   56, 63, **64**, 113

_____, and Alfred Nucci. 1989. "An Analysis of Small Business Size and Rate of Discontinuance." *Journal of Small Business Management*, Vol.27 (October 1989), pp. 1-7.

44, **45**, 119

Bearse, Peter. 1983. *An Econometric Analysis of Minority Entrepreneurship.* Washington, D.C.: U.S. Department of Commerce, Minority Business Development Agency.

57

_____. 1984. "An Econometric Analysis of Black Entrepreneurship." *The Review of Black Political Economy*, Vol. 12 (Spring 1984), pp. 111-34.

34, **40**

Bonacich, Edna, and John Modell. 1980. *The Economic Basis of Ethnic Solidarity: Small Business in the Japanese American Community.* Berkeley: University of California Press.

88

Bonacich, Edna, and Ivan Light. 1988. *Immigrant Entrepreneurs: Koreans in Los Angeles, 1965-1982.* Berkeley: University of California Press.

83, **90**

Bradford, William. 1990. "Wealth, Assests, and Income in Black Households." Afro-American Studies Program Working Paper, Vol. 1, No. 1 (February 1990), University of Maryland.

58

Brimmer, Andrew. 1966. "The Negro in the National Economy." In John David, ed., *American Negro Reference Book.* Englewood Cliffs, N.J.: Prentice-Hall.

6, **10**

_____. 1968. "Desegregation and Negro Leadership." In Eli Ginsberg, ed., *Business Leadership and the Negro Crisis.* New York: McGraw-Hill.

6, **10**

_____. 1971. "Small Business and Economic Development in the Negro Community." In Edwin Epstein and David Hampton, eds., *Black Americans and White Business*. Encino, Calif.: Dickinson Publishing.

6, **12**, 13, 15

_____, and Henry Terrell. 1971. "The Economic Potential of Black Capitalism." *Public Policy*, Vol. 19 (Spring 1971), pp. 289-308.

6, **12**, 13

Browne, Robert. 1971. "Cash Flows in a Ghetto Economy." *The Review of Black Political Economy*, Vol. 1 (Spring 1971), pp. 28-39.

6, **16**

Caplovitz, David. 1973. *The Merchants of Harlem: A Study of Small Business in the Black Community*. Beverly Hills, Calif.: Sage Publications.

6, **9**

Chen, Gavin, and John Cole. 1988. "The Myths, Facts, and Theories of Ethnic Small-Scale Enterprise Financing." *The Review of Black Political Economy*, Vol. 16 (Spring 1988), pp. 111-23.

56, **67**

Cole, John, Alfred Edwards, Earl Hamilton, and Lucy Reuben. 1985. "Black Banks: A Survey and Analysis of the Literature." *The Review of Black Political Economy*, Vol. 14 (Summer 1985), pp. 29-50.

4

Comptroller General of the United States. 1981. *The SBA 8 (a) Program: A Promise Unfulfilled*. Washington, D.C.: General Accounting Office.

19, **26**

DETAS (Development Through Applied Science). 1983. *New Perspectives on Minority Business Development*. Washington, D.C.: U.S. Department of Commerce, Minority Business Development Agency.

56, **59**, 116

Development Associates, Inc. 1987. "Attitudes and Inclinations of Minority Youth Toward Business Ownership." Unpublished report submitted to the U.S. Department of Commerce, Minority Business Development Agency.   83, **92**

Dominguez, John. 1976. *Capital Flows in Minority Areas.* Lexington, Mass.: Lexington Books.   19, **22**

Du Bois, W.E.B. 1899. *The Philadelphia Negro: A Social Study.* Philadelphia: University of Pennsylvania Press. (Reprinted in 1967 by Schocken Books.)   105

Edelstein, Robert.1975. "Improving the Selection of Credit Risks: An Analysis of a Commercial Bank Minority Lending Program." *Journal of Finance*, Vol. 30 (March 1975), pp. 38-55.   56, **64**

Elliehausen, Gregory, Glenn Canner, and Robert Avery. 1984a. "Survey of Consumer Finances, 1983." *Federal Reserve Bulletin*, Vol. 70 (September, 1984), pp. 679-92.   **58**

_____. 1984b. "Survey of Consumer Finances 1983: A Second Report." *Federal Reserve Bulletin*, Vol. 70 (December 1984), pp. 857-68.   **58**

Evans, David. 1987. "The Relationship Between Firm Growth, Size and Age: Estimates for 100 Manufacturing Industries." *The Journal of Industrial Economics*, Vol. 35 (June 1987), pp. 567-82.   44, **45**

_____, and Linda Leighton. 1989. "Some Empirical Aspects of Entrepreneurship." *American Economic Review*, Vol. 79 (June 1989), pp. 519-35.   44, **46**

Farmer, Richard T. 1968. "Black Businessmen in Indiana." *Indiana Business Review*, Vol. 43 (November 1968), pp. 12-13.   5, **8**, 11

Fleming, G. James, and Bernice Sheldon. 1938. "Fine Food for Philadelphia." *The Crisis*, Vol. 45 (April 1938), pp. 107-16.

108

Foley, Eugene. 1966. "The Negro Businessman: In Search of a Tradition." In Talcott Parsons and Kenneth Clark, eds., *The Negro American*. Boston: Houghton Mifflin.

5, **8**

Fratoe, Frank. 1984. "Abstracts of the Sociological Literature on Minority Business Ownership."

4

_____. 1988. "Social Capital and Small Business Owners." *The Review of Black Political Economy*, Vol. 16 (Spring 1988), pp. 33-50.

34, **43**, 119

_____, and Ronald Meeks. 1988. *Business Participation Rates and Self-Employment Incomes: An Analysis of the 50 Largest Ancestry Groups*. Los Angeles: UCLA Center for Afro-American Studies.

34, **37**, 114

Gilbreath, Kent. 1973. *Red Capitalism: An Analysis of the Navajo Economy*. Norman, Oklahoma: University of Oklahoma Press.

6, **9**

Granville Corporation. 1982. "A Longitudinal Analysis of Minority Business Enterprises Participating in the Local Public Works Program." Unpublished report submitted to the Economic Development Administration (December 1982).

19, **28**

Handy, John, and David Swinton. 1984. "The Determinants of the Rate of Growth of Black-Owned Businesses." *The Review of Black Political Economy*, Vol. 12 (Spring 1984), pp. 85-110.

73, 113

Harmon, J., Arnett Lindsay, and Carter Woodson. 1929. *The Negro as Businessman*. College Park, Md.: McGrath Publishing.

108

Harris, Abram. 1936. *The Negro as Capitalist*. Philadelphia: American Academy of Political and Social Science.   105, 109

Holsey, Albon. 1938. "Seventy-Five Years of Negro Business." *The Crisis*, Vol. 45 (July 1938), pp. 231-47.   109

Jaynes, Gerald, and Robin Williams, eds. 1989. *A Common Destiny: Blacks in American Society*. Washington, D.C.: National Academy Press.   59, **81**

Johnson, Douglas. 1980. "Urban Impact Analysis of the Small Business Administration 7(a) and Economic Opportunity Loan Programs." MIT Urban and Community Impacts Discussion Paper No. 7.   19, **24**, 113

Jovanovic, Boyan. 1982. "Selection and Evolution in Industry." *Econometrica*, Vol. 50 (May 1982), pp. 649-70.   **44**

Kelsey, Carl. 1903. "The Evolution of Negro Labor," *Annals of the American Academy of Political and Social Science*, Vol. 21, pp. 59-74.   107

Klein, Richard. 1978. "SBA's Business Loan Programs." *Atlanta Economic Review*, Vol. 23 (September-October 1978), pp. 28-37.   19, **23**, 25, 113

Light, Ivan. 1972. *Ethnic Enterprise in America*. Berkeley: University of California Press.   **84**, 86

Markwalder, Donald. 1981. "The Potential for Black Business." *The Review of Black Political Economy*, Vol. 11 (Spring 1981), pp. 303-12.   **17**, 112

Myrdal, Gunnar. 1944. *The American Dilemma*. New York: Harper and Brothers.   109

Oakland, William, Frederick Sparrow, and H. Stettler. 1971. "Ghetto Multipliers: A Case Study of Hough." *Journal of Regional Science*, Vol. 11 (July 1971), pp. 337-45.   17

Osborne, Alfred. 1976. "The Welfare Effects of Black Capitalists on the Black Community." *The Review of Black Political Economy*, Vol. 6 (Summer 1976) pp. 477-84.   **27**

_____, and Michael Granfield. 1976. "The Potential of Black Capitalism in Perspective." *Public Policy*, Vol. 24 (Fall 1976), pp. 529-44.   19, **27**

Pierce,   Joseph. 1947. *Negro Business and Business Education.* New York: Harper and Brothers.   5, **6**, 8, 11, 107

Ransom, Roger, and Richard Sutch. 1977. *One Kind of Freedom.* New York: Cambridge University Press.   107

Reid, John. 1982. "Black America in   the   1980s." *Population Bulletin*, Vol. 37 (December 1983), pp. 1-39.   **51**

Schaffer, Richard. 1973. *Income Flows in Urban Poverty Areas: A Comparison of the Community Income Accounts of Bedford-Stuyvesant and Borough Park.* Lexington, Mass.: Lexington Books.   72, **76**

Simms, Margaret C., and Lynn Burbridge. 1986. *Minority Business Formation and Failure by Industry and by Location.* Washington, D.C.:   U.S. Department of Commerce, Minority Business Development Agency.   68, **71**, 112

Small Business Administration. 1971. *SBA: What It Is...What It Does.* Washington, D.C.: Government Printing Office.   21

Small Business Administration, 8(a) Review Board. 1978. "Report and Recommendations on the Section 8(a) Program for A. Vernon Weaver, Administrator." Washington, D.C.   19, **26**

Stevens, Richard. 1984. "Measuring Minority Business Formation and Failure." *The Review of Black Political Economy*, Vol. 12 (Spring 1984), pp. 71-84.   34, **41**, 112

Suggs, Robert. 1986. "Recent Changes in Black-Owned Business." Working paper, Joint Center for Political Studies. Washington, D.C.   34, **38**, 113

Swinton, David, and John Handy. 1983. *The Determinants of the Growth of Black-Owned Businesses: A Preliminary Analysis*. Washington, D.C.: U.S. Department of Commerce, Minority Business Development Agency.   **49**, 113

Tabb, William. 1972. "Viewing Minority Economic Development as a Problem in Political Economy." *American Economic Review*, Vol. 62 (May 1972), pp. 31-8.   **27**

_____. 1979. "What Ever Happened to Black Economic Development?" *The Review of Black Political Economy*, Vol. 9 (Summer 1979), pp. 392-415.   **27**

Terrell, Henry. 1971. "Wealth Accumulation of Black and White Families." *Journal of Finance*, Vol. 26 (May 1971).   **57**, 58

Trent, William. 1984. "Equity Considerations in Higher Education: Race and Sex Differences in Degree Attainment and Major Field from 1976 through 1981." *American Journal of Education*, Vol. 41 (May 1984), pp. 280-305.   **51**

U.S. Department of Commerce, Economic Development Administration. 1980. *Local Public Works Program: Final Report.* Washington, D.C.

Waldinger, Roger. 1986. *Through the Eye of the Needle: Immigrants and Enterprise in New York's Garment Trades.* New York: New York University Press.

Walker, Juliet. 1986. "Racism, Slavery and Free Enterprise: Black Entrepreneurship in the United States before the Civil War." *Business History Review,* Vol. 60 (Autumn 1986), pp. 343-82.

White, Lawrence. 1982. "The Determinants of the Relative Importance of Small Business." *The Review of Economics and Statistics,* Vol. 54 (February 1982), pp. 42-9.

Woolf, Arthur. 1986. "Market Structure and Minority Presence: Black-Owned Firms in Manufacturing." *The Review of Black Political Economy,* Vol. 14 (Spring 1986), pp. 79-89.

Title Index
by Subject

Note: Review entries in this volume are indicated in boldface.

Part 1. Early Studies of Minority-Owned Businesses

Negro Business and Business Education, by Joseph Pierce (1947) **No. 1**

"The Negro Businessman: In Search of a Tradition," by Eugene Foley (1966) **No. 2**

"The Negro in the National Economy," by Andrew Brimmer (1966) **No. 6a**

"The Potential for Black Business," by Don Markwalder (1981) **No. 12**

"The Potential for Black Business: A Comment," by Timothy Bates (1983) **No. 13**

"The Potential of Black Capitalism," by Timothy Bates (1973) **No. 7**

Red Capitalism: An Analysis of the Navajo Economy, by Kent Gilbreath (1973) **No. 5**

"Small Business and Economic Development in the Negro Community," by Andrew Brimmer (1971) **No. 8b**

Government Programs to Assist Minority Business

"Black Entrepreneurship and Government Programs," by Timothy Bates (1981) **No. 25**

Capital Flows in Minority Areas, by John Dominguez (1976) **No. 16**

Financing Black Economic Development, by Timothy Bates and William Bradford (1979) **No. 20**

"Financing Black Enterprises," by Timothy Bates (1974) **No. 15**

"Government as Financial Intermediary for Minority Entrepreneurs," by Timothy Bates (1975) **No. 14**

"What Ever Happened to Black Economic Development?" by William Tabb (1979) **No. 22b**

Part 2. Modern Quantitative Studies
Minority-Owned Businesses

Business Participation Rates and Self-Employment Incomes: An Analysis of the 50 Largest Ancestry Groups, by Frank Fratoe and Ronald Meeks (1988) **No. 27**

"An Econometric Analysis of Black Entrepreneurship," by Peter Bearse (1984). **No. 30**

"Measuring Minority Business Formation and Failure," by Richard Stevens (1984) **No. 31**

"Recent Changes in Black-Owned Business," by Robert Suggs (1986) **No. 28**

"Self-Employed Minorities: Traits and Trends," by Timothy Bates (1987) **No. 26**

"Social Capital and Small Business Owners," by Frank Fratoe (1988) **No. 32**

"Traditional and Emerging Lines of Black Enterprise," by Timothy Bates (1992, forthcoming) **No. 29**

Small Business in General

"An Analysis of Small Business Size and Rate of Discontinuance," by Timothy Bates and Alfred Nucci (1989) **No. 34b**

"The Determinants of the Relative Importance of Small Business," by Lawrence White (1982) **No. 38**

"Entrepreneur Factor Inputs and Small Business Longevity," by Timothy Bates (1989) **No. 36**

"Entrepreneur Human Capital Inputs and Small Business Longevity," by Timothy Bates (1990) **No. 37**

"The Relationship Between Firm Growth, Size and Age: Estimates for 100 Manufacturing Industries," by David Evans (1987) **No. 34a**

"Selection and Evolution in Industry," by Boyan Jovanovic (1982) **No. 33**

Some Empirical Aspects of Entrepreneurship," by David Evans and Linda Leighton (1989) **No. 35**

The Role of Human Capital

An Analysis of Income Differentials Among Self- Employed Minorities, by Timothy Bates (1988) **No. 44**

"Black America in the 1980s," by John Reid (1983) **No. 42a**

"Characteristics of Minorities Who Are Entering Self-Employment," by Timothy Bates (1986) **No. 41**

The Determinants of the Growth of Black-Owned Businesses: A Preliminary Analysis, by David Swinton and John Handy (1983) **No. 39**

"Entrepreneur Human Capital Endowments and Minority Business Viability," by Timothy Bates (1985) **No. 40**

"Equity Considerations in Higher Education: Race and Sex Differences in Degree Attainment and Major Field from 1976 through 1981," by William Trent (1984) **No. 42b**

"Why Black Firms Fail," by Timothy Bates (1992, forthcoming) **No. 45**

Seventh Annual Status Report, (American Council on Education, 1988) **No. 43**

The Role of Financial Capital

"Analysis of a Commercial Bank Minority Lending Program: Comment," by Timothy Bates and Donald Hester (1977) **No. 53b**

"Capital Issues and Minority-Owned Business," by Faith Ando (1988) **No. 52**

An Econometric Analysis of Minority Entrepreneurship, by Peter Bearse (1983) **No. 47**

"Why Black Firms Fail," by Timothy Bates (1992, forthcoming) **No. 51**

"Improving the Selection of Credit Risks: An Analysis of a Commercial Bank Minority Lending Program," by Robert Edelstein (1975) **No. 53a**

"The Myths, Facts, and Theories of Ethnic Small-Scale Enterprise Financing," by Gavin Chen and John Cole (1988) **No. 55**

New Perspectives on Minority Business Development, (Development Through Applied Science, 1983) **No. 50**

"Small Business Viability in the Urban Ghetto," by Timothy Bates (1989) **No. 54**

"Survey of Consumer Finances, 1983," by Gregory Elliehausen, Glenn Canner, and Robert Avery (1984) **No. 48a**

"Survey of Consumer Finances, 1983: A Second Report," by Gregory Elliehausen, Glenn Canner, and Robert Avery (1984) **No. 48b**

"Wealth Accumulation of Black and White Families," by Henry Terrell (1971) **No. 46**

"Wealth, Assets, and Income in Black Households," by William D. Bradford (1990) **No. 49**

Structural Barriers to Small Business Entry

"Market Structure and Minority Presence: Black-Owned Firms in Manufacturing," by Arthur Woolf (1986) **No. 57**

Minority Business Formation and Failure by Industry and by Location, by Margaret Simms and Lynn Burbridge (1986) **No. 58**

Through the Eye of the Needle: Immigrants and Enterprise in New York's Garment Trades, by Roger Waldinger (1986) **No. 56**

Access to Markets, Job Creation, and Related Issues

"Firm Location and Bank Redlining," by Timothy Bates (1992, forthcoming) **No. 66**

"Public Policy That Would Make A Difference," by Timothy Bates (1992, forthcoming) **No. 64**

"The Determinants of the Rate of Growth of Black-Owned Businesses," by John Handy and David Swinton (1984) **No. 59**

"Do Black-Owned Businesses Employ Minority Workers? New Evidence," by Timothy Bates (1988) **No. 65**

Income Flows in Urban Poverty Areas: A Comparison of the Community Income Accounts of Bedford-Stuyvesant and Borough Park, by Richard Schaffer (1973) **No. 63**

"The Economic Dynamics of the Urban Ghetto," by Timothy Bates and Daniel Fusfeld (1984) **No. 62**

"Urban Economic Transformation and Minority Business Opportunities," by Timothy Bates (1984-85) **No. 61**

"The Urban Ghetto Milieu," by Timothy Bates (1992, forthcoming) **No. 60**

The Impact of Black Elected Officials on Black Business Development

"Black Mayors and the Impact of Set-Asides," by Timothy Bates (1992, forthcoming) **No. 68**

A Common Destiny: Blacks in American Society, Gerald Jaynes and Robin Williams, eds. (1989) **No. 67**

Asian and Hispanic Self-Employment

"Attitudes and Inclinations of Minority Youth Toward Business Ownership," (Development Associates, Inc., 1987) **No. 75**

"The Changing Nature of Minority Business: A Comparative Analysis of Asian, Nonminority, and Black-Owned Businesses," by Timothy Bates (1989) **No. 71**

The Economic Basis of Ethnic Solidarity: Small Business in the Japanese American Community, by Edna Bonacich and John Modell (1980) **No. 72**

"Ethnic Advantage and Minority Business Development," by Howard Aldrich, Trevor Jones, and David McEvoy (1984) **No. 74**

Ethnic Enterprise in America, by Ivan Light (1972) **No. 69**

Immigrant Entrepreneurs: Koreans in Los Angeles 1965-1982, by Edna Bonacich and Ivan Light (1988) **No. 73**

Throught the Eye of the Needle: Immigrants and Enterprise in New York's Garment Trades, by Roger Waldinger (1986) **No. 70**

Joint Center Board of Governors

Joint Center Books of Related Interest

Banking on Black Enterprise: The Potential of Emerging Firms for Revitalizing Urban Economies, by Timothy Bates (1992, forthcoming)

Moving Up With Baltimore: Creating Career Ladders for Blacks in the Private Sector, by the Joint Center Research Staff (1991)

Minorities and Privatization: Economic Mobility at Risk, by Robert Suggs (1990)

Minorities and the Labor Market: Twenty Years of Misguided Policy, by Richard McGahey and John Jeffries (1985)

For ordering information, contact University Press of America, 4720 Boston Way, Lanham, Maryland 20706 (tel. 301/459-3366)